McDougal Littell

ECONOMICS
Concepts and Choices

Reading Study Guide

Warning: Permission is hereby granted to teachers to reprint or photocopy in classroom quantities the pages or sheets in this work that carry the following copyright notice: Copyright © McDougal Littell/Houghton Mifflin Company. These pages are designed to be reproduced by teachers for use in their classes with accompanying McDougal Littell material, provided each copy made shows the copyright notice. Such copies may not be sold, and further distribution is expressly prohibited. Except as authorized above, prior written permission must be obtained from McDougal Littell to reproduce or transmit this work or portions thereof in any other form or by any electronic or mechanical means, including any information storage or retrieval system, unless expressly permitted by federal copyright law. Address inquiries to Supervisor, Rights and Permissions, McDougal Littell, P.O. Box 1667, Evanston, IL 60204.

ISBN-13: 978-0-618-81528-9
ISBN-10: 0-618-81528-5

Copyright © McDougal Littell, a division of Houghton Mifflin Company.

1 2 3 4 5 6 7 8 9 — QVK — 12 11 10 09 08 07

McDougal Littell
A HOUGHTON MIFFLIN COMPANY
Evanston, Illinois • Boston • Dallas

ISBN-10: 0–618–81528–7

ISBN 978-0-618-81528-9

12 13 0982 15 14 13
4500403737

Contents

Name _____ Date _____

READING STUDY GUIDE
Scarcity: The Basic Economic Problem

- **Before You Learned** Economics is the study of how individuals and societies satisfy their unlimited wants with limited resources.

- **Now You Will Learn** The economic problem of scarcity guides economists to ask and answer basic questions about the economy.

AS YOU READ Take notes to help you understand why scarcity is the central concept of economics.

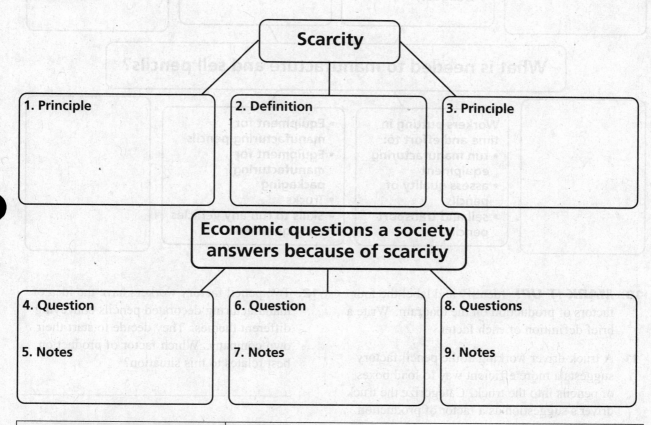

Scarcity

1. Principle

2. Definition

3. Principle

Economic questions a society answers because of scarcity

4. Question

5. Notes

6. Question

7. Notes

8. Questions

9. Notes

VOCABULARY HUNT
Circle each term where it appears in your notes and be sure you understand its meaning. If a term does not appear, write it beside the box where it best belongs.

scarcity	consumer
goods	producer
services	factors of production

CHAPTER 1

APPLICATION

- Assessment of market for pencils
- Drive to invest in the manufacture of writing implements and to market them creatively

- Wood
- Graphite
- Brass
- Rubber
- Cardboard

What is needed to manufacture and sell pencils?

Workers putting in time and effort to:
- run manufacturing equipment
- assess quality of pencils
- sell and transport pencils

- Equipment for manufacturing pencils
- Equipment for manufacturing packaging
- Trucks
- Skills to run any vehicles and equipment

10. **MARK IT UP!** Identify and label the four factors of production on the diagram. Write a brief definition of each factor.

11. A truck driver working at the pencil factory suggests a more efficient way to load boxes of pencils into the truck. Categorize the truck driver's suggestion as a factor of production.

_____

_____

_____

12. Two pencil factory workers have the idea of manufacturing decorated pencils conveying different themes. They decide to start their own company. Which factor of production best relates to this situation?

_____

_____

Copyright © McDougal Littell/Houghton Mifflin Company.

SECTION 2

READING STUDY GUIDE

Economic Choice Today: Opportunity Cost

- **Before You Learned** The economic problem of scarcity guides economists to ask and answer basic questions about the economy.

- **Now You Will Learn** People consider several different factors, including incentives, utility, benefits, and costs when they make economic choices.

AS YOU READ Take notes to help you understand how people make economic choices.

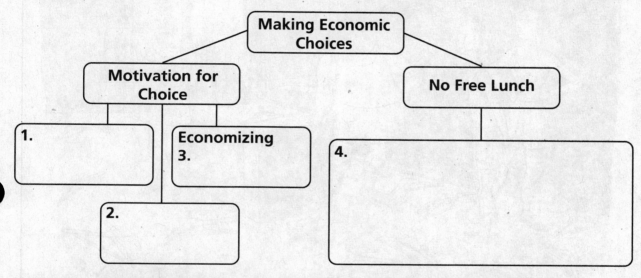

	Trade-off	Opportunity cost
Definition	5.	7.
Example	6.	8.

VOCABULARY HUNT

Circle each term where it appears in your notes and be sure you understand its meaning. If a term does not appear, write it beside the box where it best belongs.

incentives   trade-off

utility   opportunity cost

economize

ECONOMIC CHOICE TODAY: OPPORTUNITY COST, *CONTINUED*

APPLICATION

"Most successful suit sale we ever had, I should say."

9. **MARK IT UP!** Reread your notes on "Trade-Offs and Opportunity Cost." Highlight the key vocabulary terms. Think about how these terms relate to the cartoon.

10. How does the cartoon show that the suit sale was extremely successful?

_____

_____

_____

11. What is the opportunity cost of the sales force's decision to sell the last four suits?

_____

_____

12. Does the sales force seem satisfied with the trade-off they have made? Use details of the cartoon to explain your answer.

_____

_____

_____

SECTION
3

READING STUDY GUIDE
Analyzing Production Possibilities

- **Before You Learned** People consider several different factors, including incentives, utility, benefits, and costs when they make economic choices.

- **Now You Will Learn** Economists study economic choices using simplified models, such as the production possibilities curve (PPC).

Take notes to help you understand why and how production possibilities curves are constructed and used.

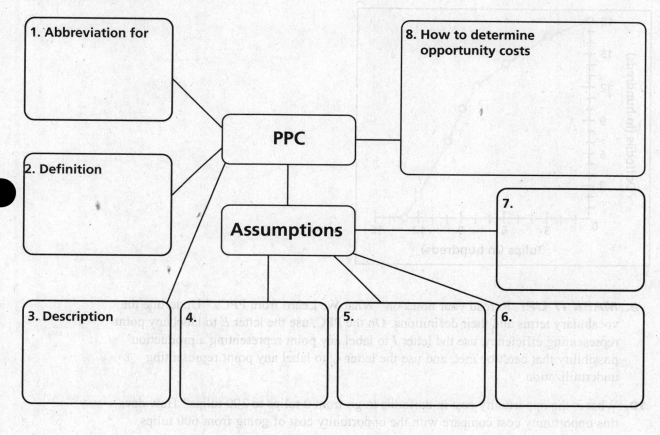

1. Abbreviation for

2. Definition

3. Description

PPC

Assumptions

8. How to determine opportunity costs

7.

4.

5.

6.

ANALYZING PRODUCTION POSSIBILITIES, *CONTINUED*

VOCABULARY HUNT Circle each term where it appears in your notes and be sure you understand its meaning. If a term does not appear, reread the section and add information about the term to your notes.	economic model law of opportunity cost efficiency underutilization

APPLICATION

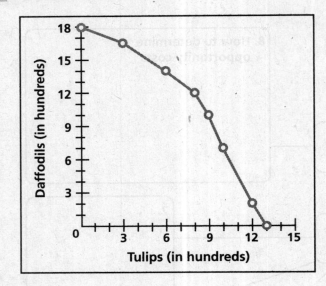

9. **MARK IT UP!** Reread your notes on "What We Learn from PPCs." Underline the vocabulary terms and their definitions. On the PPC, use the letter *E* to label any point representing efficiency, use the letter *I* to label any point representing a production possibility that can't be met, and use the letter *U* to label any point representing underutilization.

10. What is the opportunity cost in daffodils to go from 0 tulips to 300 tulips? How does this opportunity cost compare with the opportunity cost of going from 600 tulips to 900 tulips?

_____

_____

SECTION 4
READING STUDY GUIDE
The Economist's Toolbox

- **Before You Learned** Economists study economic choices using simplified models, such as the production possibilities curve (PPC).

- **Now You Will Learn** Economists work with a variety of data, including data related to microeconomics, macroeconomics, positive economics, and normative economics.

AS YOU READ Take notes to help you understand how economist display data and which types of data are collected in the different branches of economics.

Concept	Similarities	Differences
Statistics vs. economic models	1.	2.
Line graphs vs. bar graphs vs. pie graphs	3.	4.
Microeconomics vs. macroeconomics	5.	6.
Positive economics vs. normative economics	7.	8.

VOCABULARY HUNT Circle each term where it appears in your notes and be sure you understand its meaning. For the paired terms, make sure you understand how the two terms contrast with one another.

statistics	positive economics
macroeconomics	normative
microeconomics	economics

THE ECONOMIST'S TOOLBOX, *CONTINUED*

APPLICATION

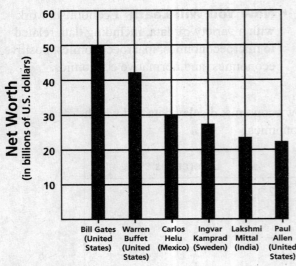

Source: Forbes, March 2006

9. **MARK IT UP!** Reread your notes on "Working with Data." Highlight information on how economists present economic data and when they use each of the different forms. Identify the main purpose of this bar graph.

10. Who was wealthier in 2006, Lakshmi Mittal, Ingvar Kamprad, or Carlos Helu?

_____

_____

_____

11. In 2006, almost half the countries in the world had gross domestic products of less than $30 billion U.S. dollars. Does this mean that some of the billionaires in this graph are wealthier individually than almost half the countries in the world? Why or why not?

_____

_____

12. Who is most likely to be interested in the data from the bar graph, a microeconomist or a macroeconomist? Explain

_____

_____

● **SECTION** **1** | READING STUDY GUIDE
Introduction to Economic Systems

- **Before You Learned** Basic economic questions each society answers include: What will be produced? How will it be produced? For whom will it be produced?

- **Now You Will Learn** The three types of economic systems each provide different answers to the basic economic questions.

AS YOU READ Take notes to help you understand the characteristics of the three main economic systems.

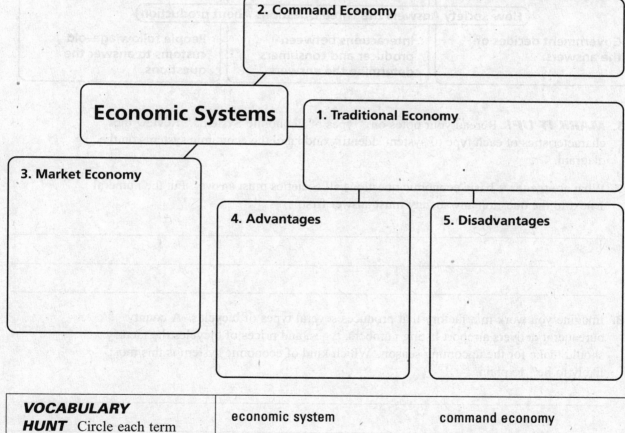

Economic Systems

2. Command Economy

1. Traditional Economy

3. Market Economy

4. Advantages

5. Disadvantages

VOCABULARY HUNT Circle each term where it appears in your notes. Check to make sure your notes include a clear definition for each term.	economic system	command economy
	traditional economy	market economy

INTRODUCTION TO ECONOMIC SYSTEMS, *CONTINUED*

APPLICATION

```
┌─────────────────────────────┐        ┌─────────────────────────────┐
│   How will it be produced?  │        │  For whom will it be produced? │
└─────────────────────────────┘        └─────────────────────────────┘

              ┌─────────────────────────────┐
              │     What will be produced?  │
              └─────────────────────────────┘
```

(How Society Answers the Three Questions About production)

| Government decides on the answers. | Interactions between producer and consumers determine the answers. | People follow age–old customs to answer the questions |

6. **MARK IT UP!** Reread your notes on "Types of Economic Systems." Review the characteristics of each type of system. Identify and label the economic systems on the diagram.

7. What are the three basic economic questions all societies must answer. Put the numeral 1 next to the question any society must answer first.

_____

_____

_____

8. Imagine you work in a factory that produces several types of bicycles. A county bureaucrat delivers a report listing numbers, types, and prices of bicycles the factory should make for the upcoming season. Which kind of economic system is this most likely to be? Explain.

_____

_____

CHAPTER 2

SECTION
2

READING STUDY GUIDE
Command Economies

- **Before You Learned** The three types of economic systems each provide different answers to the basic economic questions.

- **Now You Will Learn** Governments exert different amounts of control in different types of command economies.

AS YOU READ Take notes to help you understand command economies and how they work.

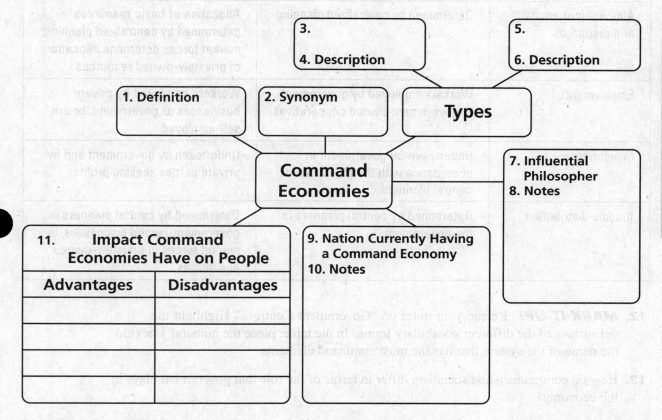

3.

4. Description

5.

6. Description

1. Definition

2. Synonym

Types

Command Economies

7. Influential Philosopher
8. Notes

11. **Impact Command Economies Have on People**

Advantages	Disadvantages

9. **Nation Currently Having a Command Economy**
10. Notes

VOCABULARY HUNT Circle each term where it appears in your notes and be sure you understand its meaning. If a term does not appear, write it beside the box where it best belongs

centrally planned economy	communism
socialism	authoritarian

CHAPTER 2

COMMAND ECONOMIES, *CONTINUED*

APPLICATION

Comparing Communism and Socialism		
	Communism	Socialism
Property rights	Resources owned by the government	Basic resources owned by government, the rest privately owned
Allocation of goods and resources	Determined by centralized planning	Allocation of basic resources determined by centralized planning; market forces determine allocation of privately-owned resources
Employment	Workers employed by government or government-owned cooperatives	Workers employed by private businesses or government, or are self-employed
Investment	Undertaken by government in accordance with the objectives of central planners	Undertaken by government and by private parties seeking profits
Income distribution	Determined by central planners in the government	Determined by central planners in government-owned businesses, by market forces in privately-owned businesses

12. **MARK IT UP!** Reread your notes on "Government Controls." Highlight the definitions of the different vocabulary terms. In the table, place the numeral 1 next to the name of the system that has the most command elements.

13. How do communism and socialism differ in terms of the role that government plays in the economy?

_____

_____

14. How do you think incentives for individuals would differ between the two systems?

_____

_____

SECTION

3 | READING STUDY GUIDE
Market Economies

- **Before You Learned** Governments exert different amounts of control in different types of command economies.

- **Now You Will Learn** To function well, market economies require the following:

protection of private property rights, voluntary exchange in markets, competition, consumer sovereignty, specialization, and minimal government involvement in most markets.

AS YOU READ Take notes to help you understand market economies and how they work.

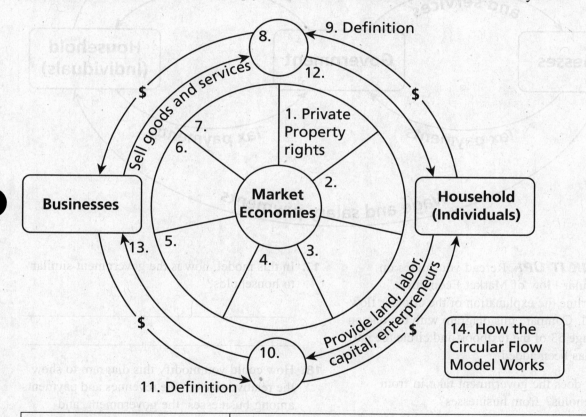

9. Definition
8.
12.
Sell goods and services
$
7.
6.
1. Private Property rights
2.
Businesses
Market Economies
Household (Individuals)
13.
5.
$
4.
3.
Provide land, labor, capital, enterpreneurs
$
10.
$
11. Definition
14. How the Circular Flow Model Works

VOCABULARY HUNT Circle each term where it appears in your notes and be sure you understand its meaning. If a term does not appear, write it beside the box where it best belongs

capitalism	product market
competition	factor market
specialization	

MARKET ECONOMIES, *CONTINUED*

APPLICATION

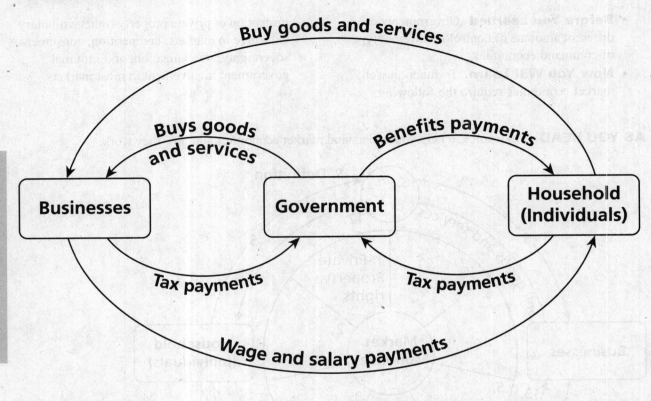

15. **MARK IT UP!** Reread your notes on "Circular Flow of Market Economies." Underline the explanation of the circular flow model. Compare this diagram with the one on the page 53 of the textbook and circle the part that has been added.

16. What does the government take in from households? from businesses?

_____

_____

_____

17. In this model, how is the government similar to households?

_____

_____

18. How could you modify this diagram to show the relative sizes of the revenues and payments among businesses, the government, and households?

_____

_____

CHAPTER 2

SECTION
4

READING STUDY GUIDE
Modern Economies in a Global Age

- **Before You Learned** To function well, market economies require the following: protection of private property rights, voluntary exchange in markets, competition, consumer sovereignty, specialization, and minimal government involvement in most markets.

- **Now You Will Learn** Modern economies include aspects of traditional, command, and market economies and, increasingly, have global ties.

AS YOU READ Take notes to help you understand modern economies and trends such economies follow.

1. Life in a Mixed Economy	2. Types of Mixed Economies	3. Trend 1	4. Trend 2

Today's Mixed Economies

Trends in Modern Economies

Modern Economies

CHAPTER 2

VOCABULARY HUNT Circle each term where it appears in your notes and be sure you've included its definition. If a term does not appear, write it beside the box where it best belongs and add a definition of the term.

mixed economy	global economy
nationalize	privatize

MODERN ECONOMIES IN A GLOBAL AGE, *CONTINUED*

APPLICATION

Country	Total Economic Activity (in billions of dollars)	Government Spending (in billions of dollars)	Government Spending as % of Total Economic Activity
Mexico	699.5	184	26
South Korea	801.2	189	24
Vietnam	44.66	12.95	29

5. **MARK IT UP!** Reread your notes on mixed economies, and review how to calculate the percent the government contributes to a nation's economy. Write the formula next to the table.

6. In terms of percentage, which government contributes the least to the country's economy?

_____

_____

7. Of the countries listed in the table, which do you think has an economy that leans the most toward a command system? Explain.

_____

_____

8. How does the economy of the country you named in question 7 compare with the economies of the other countries listed in the chart? Use numbers to support your answer.

_____

_____

Name _____ Date _____

READING STUDY GUIDE

Advantages of the Free Enterprise System

- **Before You Learned**   A market economy is an economic system based on individual choice, voluntary exchange, and private ownership of resources.
- **Now You Will Learn**   A capitalist or free enterprise system, such as the economic

system of the United States, requires open economic opportunity, legal equality, and free contracts, and depends on the profit motive as an incentive.

AS YOU READ   Take notes to help you understand the free enterprise system.

1. What it is	Places where it operates	
	2. Example & description	**3. Example & description**

Free Enterprise

How it works	
Necessary rights & freedoms	**7. Example**
4.	
5.	**8. Example**
6.	

9. Who has promoted it

10. Summary of idea

VOCABULARY HUNT Circle each term where it appears in your notes and be sure you understand its meaning. If a term does not appear, write it beside the box where it best belongs.	free enterprise system free contract
	open opportunity profit motive
	legal equality

ADVANTAGES OF THE FREE ENTERPRISE SYSTEM, *CONTINUED*

APPLICATION

"*Er—might I have a hamburger?*"

11. *MARK IT UP!* Reread your notes on "How a Free Enterprise System Works." On the cartoon, label the character representing a consumer. Circle what the business owner did that illustrates the profit motive.

12. Based on the cartoon, is the business owner's idea is currently working? Explain.

_____

_____

_____

13. In what way is the example in the cartoon similar to the example of the pet rocks?

_____

_____

_____

_____

CHAPTER 3

SECTION

2 | READING STUDY GUIDE
How Does Free Enterprise Allocate Resources?

- **Before You Learned** A capitalist or free enterprise system, such as the economic system of the United States, requires open economic opportunity, legal equality, and free contracts, and depends on the profit motive as an incentive.

- **Now You Will Learn** Consumers and producers, including the U.S. government, which takes on the role of both a consumer and a producer, determine the flow of money and resources in the free enterprise economy of the United States.

AS YOU READ Take notes to help you understand how consumers, producers, and the government each influence the allocation of resources in the U.S. economy.

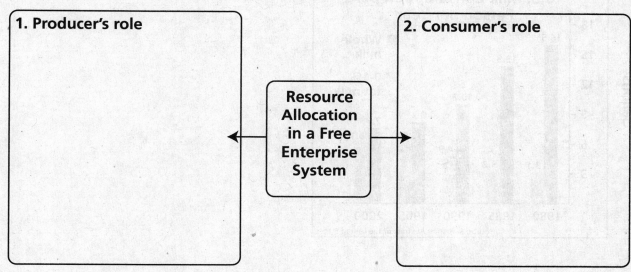

1. Producer's role

Resource Allocation in a Free Enterprise System

2. Consumer's role

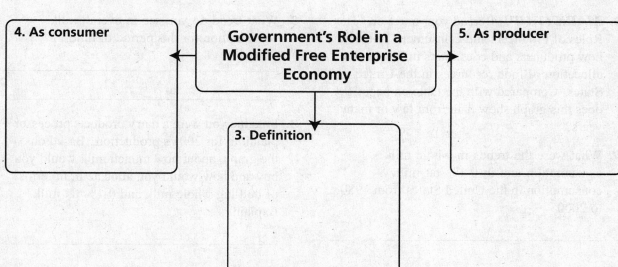

4. As consumer

Government's Role in a Modified Free Enterprise Economy

5. As producer

3. Definition

CHAPTER 3

HOW DOES FREE ENTERPRISE ALLOCATE RESOURCES?, *CONTINUED*

VOCABULARY HUNT Circle each term where it appears in your notes and be sure you understand its meaning. If a term does not appear, write it beside the box where it best belongs.	profit	modified free enterprise economy

APPLICATION

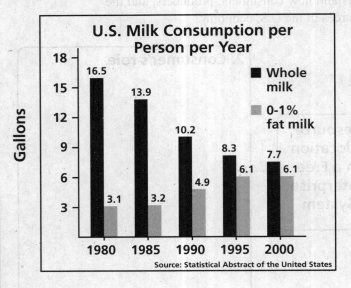

U.S. Milk Consumption per Person per Year

Gallons

- Whole milk (black)
- 0-1% fat milk (gray)

Year	Whole milk	0-1% fat milk
1980	16.5	3.1
1985	13.9	3.2
1990	10.2	4.9
1995	8.3	6.1
2000	7.7	6.1

Source: Statistical Abstract of the United States

6. **MARK IT UP!** Reread your notes on "The Roles of Producers and Consumers." Review how producers and consumers influence the allocation of food resources in the United States. Compared with the table on page 79, does this graph show data from few or many years?

7. What were the trends in whole milk consumption and in 0-1% fat milk consumption in the United States from 1980 to 2000.

_____

_____

_____

8. What trend do you see in overall milk consumption for this period of time?

_____

_____

9. Imagine you were a dairy products processor planning for 2001's production. Based on the graph, about how munch milk would you buy and how would you allocate it, in terms of bottling whole milk and 0-1% fat milk? Explain.

_____

_____

CHAPTER 3

SECTION
3

READING STUDY GUIDE
Government and Free Enterprise

- **Before You Learned** Consumers and producers, including the U.S. government, which takes on the role of both a consumer and a producer, determine the flow of money and resources in the free enterprise economy of the United States.

- **Now You Will Learn** The U.S. government addresses market failures by providing public goods and infrastructure, and it works to decrease negative externalities and increase positive externalities.

AS YOU READ Take notes to help you understand how government addresses market failures.

1. Definition

2. Free–rider problem

3. Definition and examples of public goods

Externalities

Government Dealing with Market Failures

4. Definition, examples, and possible government actions related to **negative** externalities

5. Definition, examples, and possible government actions related to **positive** externalities

VOCABULARY HUNT Circle each term where it appears in your notes and be sure you understand its meaning. If a term does not appear, write it beside the box where it best belongs.	public goods free rider	negative externality positive externality subsidy

CHAPTER 3

GOVERNMENT AND FREE ENTERPRISE, *CONTINUED*

APPLICATION

Mark It Up!

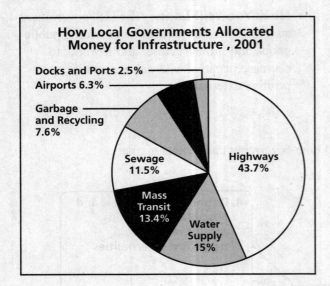

How Local Governments Allocated Money for Infrastructure , 2001

Docks and Ports 2.5%
Airports 6.3%
Garbage and Recycling 7.6%
Sewage 11.5%
Mass Transit 13.4%
Water Supply 15%
Highways 43.7%

6. Reread your notes on "Public and Private Goods." Review the characteristics of public goods and the different types of public goods. On the graph, underline the type of public good that is the graph's subject.

7. According to the graph, which type of project do local governments spend the most on? the least on?

_____

8. List three or more types of projects or services that have not been included in the graph.

_____

_____

9. What reasons can you give for both of your answers to question 7? Consider opportunity costs as part of your answer.

_____

_____

_____

10. What other sources of funding might some or all of these projects receive?

_____

_____

CHAPTER 3

SECTION 1

READING STUDY GUIDE
What Is Demand?

- **Before You Learned** Microeconomics is the study of the economic behaviors and decisions of small units, such as individuals and businesses.
- **Now You Will Learn** Demand, which is the willingness to buy something and the

ability to pay for it, can be described by demand schedules and demand curves, which illustrate the law of demand—when prices go down, quantity demanded increases, and vice versa.

VOCABULARY HUNT Circle each term where it appears in your notes and be sure you understand its meaning. If a term does not appear, reread the section and add information about the term to your notes.	demand law of demand	market demand schedule demand curve

AS YOU READ Take notes to help you understand demand, the law of demand, demand schedules, and demand curves.

1. Definition

2. Law of demand

Demand

3. Schedules

4. Curves

5. Assumptions

CHAPTER 4

WHAT IS DEMAND?, *CONTINUED*

6. Explain how Vera Wang got into the wedding gown business.

_____

7. How has her business grown and expanded?

_____

_____

APPLICATION

Mark It Up!

"*To tell you a secret, they're only marked down to discourage shoplifting. At this price it don't pay to steal them.*"

© The New Yorker Collection 1945 George Price from cartoonbank.com. All Rights Reserved.

8. Reread your notes on "The Law of Demand." Highlight the relationship between price and quantity. Draw an arrow up or down on the sign in the cartoon to show whether the storekeeper raised or lowered the price of the hats.

9. What two things does the storekeeper hope for because of the way he priced the hats?

_____

_____

10. How fashionable are the sale hats? Explain your answer using the concept of demand.

_____

SECTION 2

READING STUDY GUIDE
What Factors Affect Demand?

- **Before You Learned** Demand, which is the willingness to buy something and the ability to pay for it, can be described by demand schedules and demand curves, which illustrate the law of demand—when prices go down, quantity demanded increases and vice versa.

- **Now You Will Learn** Change in demand causes the demand curve to shift to the right with an increase in demand or to the left with a decrease in demand; changes in demand occur because of changes in income, market size, consumer taste, consumer expectations, and availability of substitutes and complements.

VOCABULARY HUNT Circle each term where it appears in your notes and be sure you understand its meaning. If a term does not appear, write it beside the box where it best belongs.	inferior goods income effect normal goods	law of diminishing marginal utility complements

AS YOU READ Take notes to help you understand changes in demand and why they occur.

Factor That Changes Demand	Reason Why Demand Changes

WHAT FACTORS AFFECT DEMAND?, *CONTINUED*

CHAPTER 4

APPLICATION

Mark It Up!

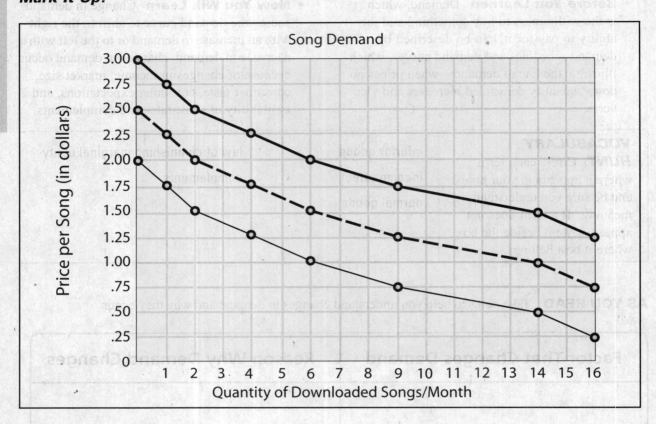

Song Demand

7. Review your notes on "Change in Demand." On the graph, label the curve that shows a demand of 14 songs per month at $1.00 per song as the normal curve.

8. There is a rumor that an online music provider is going to soon raise prices by $0.75 per song. Identify the demand curve that is most likely to result before any price hike occurs. Which factor is affecting demand? How does it work?

_____

_____

9. Imagine that CDs go on sale for one-fourth their usual price. People can record CDs on their MP3 players. Identify the demand curve for online songs that is most likely to result during the CD sale. Which factor is affecting demand? How does it work?

_____

_____

SECTION
3

READING STUDY GUIDE
What Is Elasticity of Demand?

- **Before You Learned** Change in demand causes the demand curve to shift to the right with an increase in demand or to the left with a decrease in demand; changes in demand occur because of changes in income, market size, consumer taste, consumer expectations, and availability of substitutes and complements.

- **Now You Will Learn** The relationship between price and demand depends not only on price but also on the type of good or service and whether the good or service is a necessity or not; consumer responsiveness to price change is called elasticity of demand.

AS YOU READ Take notes to help you understand elasticity of demand.

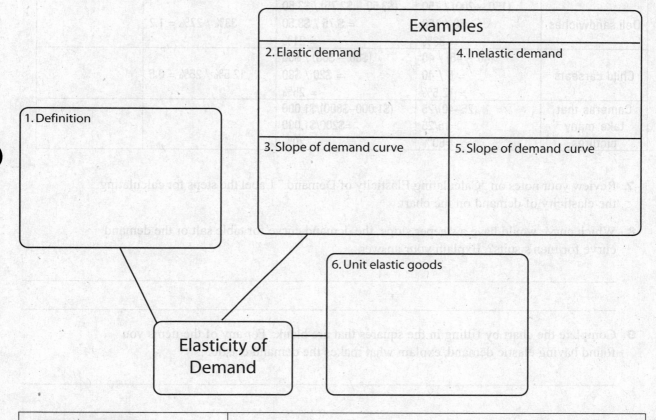

Examples	
2. Elastic demand	4. Inelastic demand
3. Slope of demand curve	5. Slope of demand curve

1. Definition

6. Unit elastic goods

Elasticity of Demand

VOCABULARY HUNT Circle each term where it appears in your notes and be sure you understand its meaning. If a term does not appear, write it beside the box where it best belongs.

elasticity of demand	total revenue test
elastic	
inelastic	

APPLICATION

Mark It Up!

Product	Percentage change in _____ (A)	Percentage change in _____ (B)	Elasticity (A) / (B) = (C)	Is demand elastic or inelastic?
Men's suits	(80 – 120) / 80 = 40 / 80 = 50%	($525 – $425) / $525 = $100 / $525 = 19%	50% / 19% = 2.6	elastic
Table salt (in 1–pound boxes)	(200 – 240) / 200 = 40 / 200 = 20%	($.52 — $.39) / $.52 = $.13 / $.52 = 25%	20% / 25% = 0.8	inelastic
Deli sandwiches	(150 – 200) / 150 = 50 / 150 = 33%	($3.50 – $2.75) / $3.50 = $.75 / $3.50 = 21%	33% / 27% = 1.2	
Child carseats	(40 – 45) / 40 = 5 / 40 = 12.5%	($80 – $60) / $80 = $20 / $80 = 25%	12.5% / 25% = 0.5	
Cameras that take many pictures	(25–40)/25 =15/25 =60%	($1,000–$800)/$1,000 =$200/$1,000 20%		

7. Review your notes on "Calculating Elasticity of Demand." Label the steps for calculating the elasticity of demand on the chart.

8. Which curve would have a steeper slope, the demand curve for table salt or the demand curve for men's suits? Explain your answer.

_____

_____

9. Complete the chart by filling in the squares that are blank. For any of the items you found having elastic demand, explain what makes the demand elastic.

_____

_____

10. For any of the items that have inelastic demand, list the factors that make the demand inelastic.

_____

_____

SECTION

1

READING STUDY GUIDE

What Is Supply?

- **Before You Learned** Demand is the willingness to buy a good or service and the ability to pay for it.

- **Now You Will Learn** Supply is willingness and ability of producers to offer goods and services for sale.

AS YOU READ Take notes to help you understand supply, the law of supply, supply schedules, and supply curves.

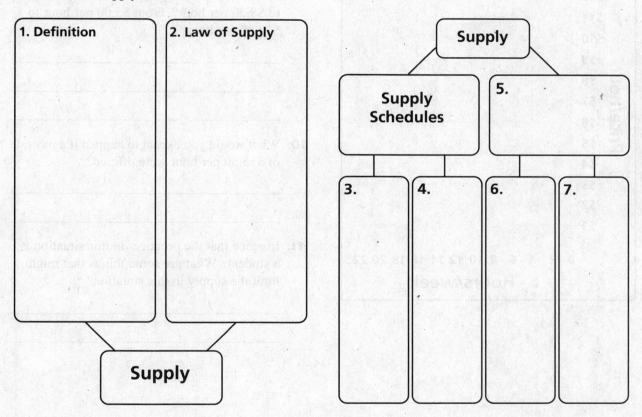

1. Definition

2. Law of Supply

Supply

Supply

Supply Schedules

5.

3.   **4.**   **6.**   **7.**

VOCABULARY HUNT Circle each term where it appears in your notes and be sure you understand its meaning. If a term does not appear, reread the section and add information about the term to your notes.

supply

law of supply

supply schedule

market supply curve

APPLICATION
Mark It Up!

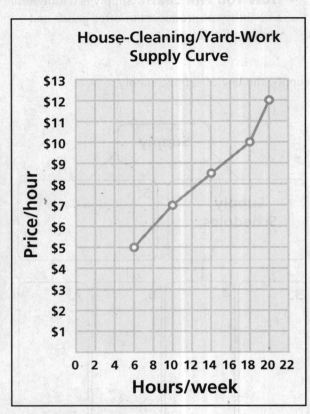

House-Cleaning/Yard-Work
Supply Curve

Price/hour — Hours/week

8. Review the definitions of supply schedule, supply curve, market supply schedule, and market supply curve. Identify whether the graph is an individual or a market supply curve, marking your answer on the graph.

9. How does the number of hours offered change when the pay rate goes from $5.00 per hour to $8.50 per hour? From $5.00 per hour to $10.00 per hour?

_____

_____

_____

10. What would you expect to happen if a pay rate of $13.50 per hour were offered?

_____

_____

11. Imagine that the producer in this situation is a student. What are some things that might limit the supply in this situation?

_____

_____

CHAPTER 5

SECTION
2

READING STUDY GUIDE
What Are the Costs of Production?

- **Before You Learned** Supply is willingness and ability of producers to offer goods and services for sale.
- **Now You Will Learn** Businesses calculate production costs and use them to figure out

how much of a good or service they can most profitably supply.

AS YOU READ Take notes to help you understand the steps in figuring out production costs and profitability.

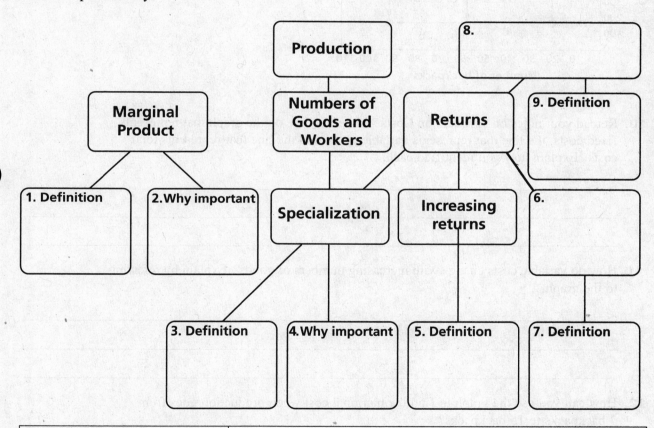

VOCABULARY HUNT Circle each term where it appears in your notes and be sure you understand its meaning. If a term does not appear, write it beside the box where it best belongs.

marginal product	diminishing returns
increasing returns	marginal revenue

CHAPTER 5

WHAT ARE THE COSTS OF PRODUCTION?, *CONTINUED*

APPLICATION

Mark It Up!

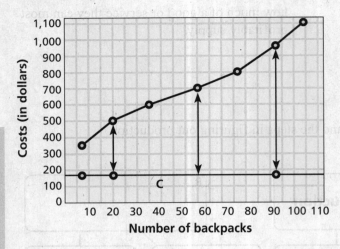

Number of backpacks

10. Reread your notes on "Production Costs." Label the line on the graph that represents fixed costs, the line that represents variable costs, and the line that represents total costs. Explain how you identified each.

_____

_____

_____

11. How do variable costs change with increasing numbers of goods? Explain by referring to the graph.

_____

_____

_____

12. How can you use the graph to find the marginal cost when production goes from 7 backpacks to 15 backpacks?

_____

_____

_____

Copyright © McDougal Littell/Houghton Mifflin Company.

CHAPTER 5

SECTION

3

READING STUDY GUIDE

What Factors Affect Supply?

- **Before You Learned** Businesses calculate production costs and use them to figure out how much of a good or service they can most profitably supply.
- **Now You Will Learn** Change in supply causes the supply curve to shift to the right

with an increase in supply or to the left with a decrease in supply; changes in supply occur because of changes in input costs, productivity, technology, producer expectation, or number of producers, or due to government action.

AS YOU READ Take notes to help you understand changes in supply and why they occur.

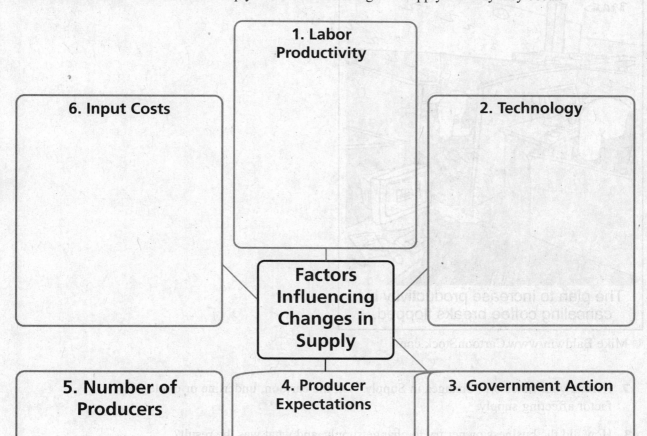

1. Labor Productivity

6. Input Costs

2. Technology

Factors Influencing Changes in Supply

5. Number of Producers

4. Producer Expectations

3. Government Action

CHAPTER 5

WHAT FACTORS AFFECT SUPPLY?, *CONTINUED*

VOCABULARY HUNT In your notes circle each term. Be sure you understand its meaning.	change in supply	excise tax
	input costs	labor productivity

APPLICATION
Mark It Up!

The plan to increase productivity by canceling coffee breaks flopped.

© Mike Baldwin/www.CartoonStock.com

7. Reread your notes on "Changes in Supply." On the cartoon, underline or circle the factor affecting supply.

8. How did the business owner try to change supply, and what was the result?

_____

9. How would the supply curve change because of the situation in the cartoon?

_____

10. What is the main technique the cartoonist uses to deliver the message? Explain.

_____

SECTION
4 | READING STUDY GUIDE
What Is Elasticity of Supply?

- **Before You Learned** Change in supply causes the supply curve to shift to the right with an increase in supply or to the left with a decrease in supply; changes in supply occur because of changes in input costs, productivity, technology, producer expectation, number of producers, or due to government action.

- **Now You Will Learn** The relationship between supply and price depends not only on price but also on production processes and other factors; producer responsiveness to price change is called elasticity of supply

AS YOU READ Take notes to help you understand elasticity of supply.

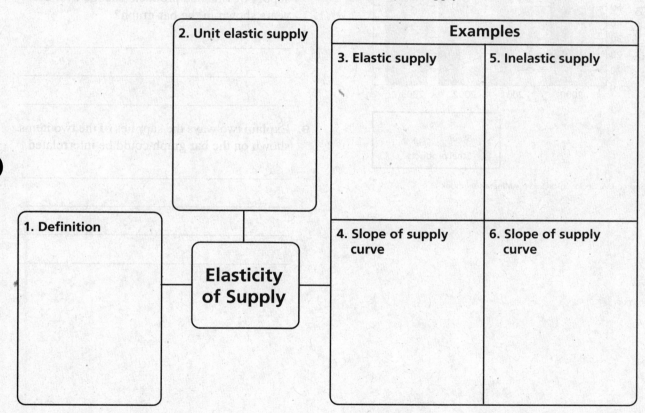

2. Unit elastic supply

Examples

3. Elastic supply

5. Inelastic supply

1. Definition

Elasticity of Supply

4. Slope of supply curve

6. Slope of supply curve

VOCABULARY HUNT Circle the term where it appears in your notes and be sure you understand its meaning. If the term does not appear, reread the section and add the term and information about the term to your notes

elasticity of supply

CHAPTER 5

WHAT IS ELASTICITY OF SUPPLY?, *CONTINUED*

APPLICATION

Mark It Up!

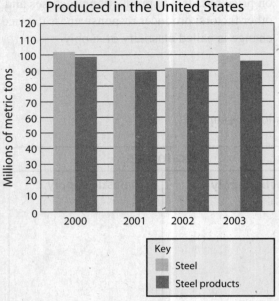

Steel and Steel Products
Produced in the United States

Millions of metric tons

Key
Steel
Steel products

Source: U.S. Geological Survey Minerals Yearbook

7. Reread your notes on "What Affects Elasticity of Supply." On the bar graph, label the raw material. On the line below, list some examples of products the bar graph could include.

_____

_____

8. How did the supply of raw material and the supply of finished products change over the years shown in the bar graph?

_____

_____

_____

9. Explain two ways the supplies of the two items shown on the bar graph could be interrelated.

_____

_____

_____

_____

Name _____   Date _____

Seeking Equilibrium: Supply and Demand

- **Before You Learned** Demand is a consumer's willingness to buy a good or service along with the ability to pay for it; supply is a producer's willingness and ability to produce and sell a good or service.

- **Now You Will Learn** Producers and consumers interact to determine equilibrium price, which can change with changes in supply and changes in demand, sometimes leading to surpluses or shortages.

AS YOU READ   Take notes to help you understand the interaction between supply, demand, and equilibrium price.

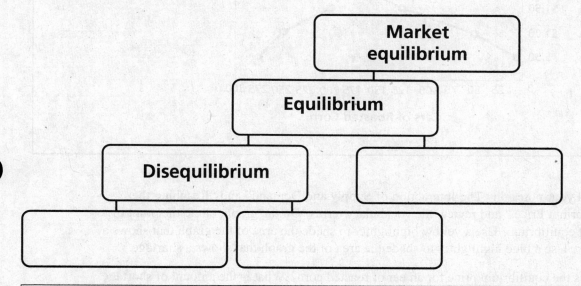

VOCABULARY HUNT Circle each term where it appears in your notes and be sure you understand its meaning. If a term does not appear, write it beside the box where it best belongs.

market equilibrium   surplus

equilibrium price   shortage

                                   disequilibrium

CHAPTER 6

SEEKING EQUILIBRIUM: SUPPLY AND DEMAND, *CONTINUED*

APPLICATION
Mark It Up!

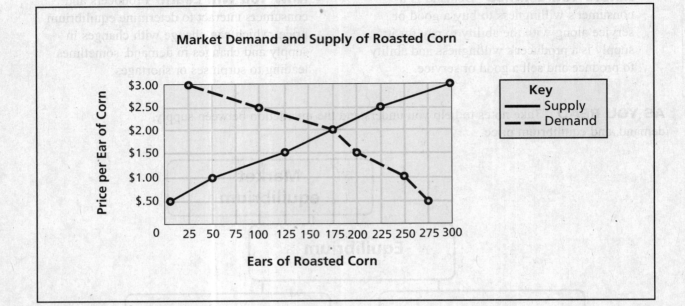

Market Demand and Supply of Roasted Corn

Key
— Supply
– – Demand

Price per Ear of Corn

$3.00
$2.50
$2.00
$1.50
$1.00
$.50

0 25 50 75 100 125 150 175 200 225 250 275 300

Ears of Roasted Corn

1. Reread your notes on "The Interaction of Supply and Demand" and "Reaching the Equilibrium Price," and review the vocabulary terms. On the graph, circle the point of market equilibrium. Use a yellow highlighter to shade the area of the graph that shows a surplus. Use a blue highlighter to shade the area of the graph that shows a shortage.

2. What is the equilibrium price for an ear of roasted corn? What is the amount of shortage when the price of an ear of corn is $1.50? What is the amount of surplus when the price of an ear of corn is $2.50?

_____

_____

3. If the city raised the license fee for food vendors, how would this change the graph?

_____

_____

4. If a food critic praised the food sold at city street fairs, how would this change the graph?

_____

_____

CHAPTER 6

Name _____ Date _____

2 READING STUDY GUIDE
Prices as Signals and Incentives

- **Before You Learned** Producers and consumers interact to determine equilibrium price, which can change with changes in supply and changes in demand, sometimes leading to surpluses or shortages.

- **Now You Will Learn** Prices act as signals and incentives to both producers and consumers, and the price system provides equality, independence, flexibility, and efficiency in a market economy.

AS YOU READ   Take notes to help you understand the how the price system works and how prices act as signals and incentives to both producers and consumers.

1. Definition	3.	4.

Competitive Pricing

Characteristics of the Price Sytem in a Market Economy

2. Example	6.	5.

VOCABULARY HUNT Circle each term where it appears in your notes and be sure you understand its meaning. If a term does not appear, write it beside the box where it best belongs.

competitive pricing   incentive

CHAPTER 6

PRICES AS SIGNALS AND INCENTIVES, *CONTINUED*

APPLICATION
Mark It Up!

© Harley Schwadron/www.CartoonStock.com

7. Reread your notes on "How the Price System Works" and "Price Motivates Producers and Consumers." Label the people in the cartoon as either producers or consumers.

8. What is the customary relationship between the size of a product and its price? How does this help explain the ironic humor of the cartoon?

   _____

   _____

   _____

CHAPTER 6

Intervention in the Price System

- **Before You Learned** Prices act as signals and incentives to both producers and consumers, and the price system provides equality, independence, flexibility, and efficiency in a market economy.
- **Now You Will Learn** Government and nonprofit institutions sometimes impose price ceilings to keep the cost of items below the equilibrium price or price floors to keep the cost of a good or service above the equilibrium price. In times of national emergency, the government may institute rationing to allocate goods.

AS YOU READ Take notes to help you understand price ceilings, price floors, and rationing and the economic effects they have.

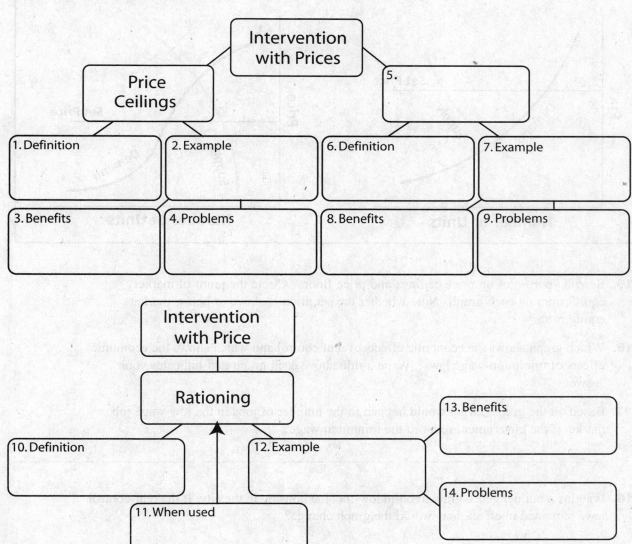

Intervention with Prices

Price Ceilings

5.

1. Definition

2. Example

6. Definition

7. Example

3. Benefits

4. Problems

8. Benefits

9. Problems

Intervention with Price

Rationing

10. Definition

12. Example

11. When used

13. Benefits

14. Problems

INTERVENTION IN THE PRICE SYSTEM, *CONTINUED*

VOCABULARY HUNT Circle each term where it appears in your notes and be sure you understand its meaning. If a term does not appear, write it beside the box where it best belongs.	price ceiling	rationing
	price floor	black market
	minimum wage	

APPLICATION
Mark It Up!

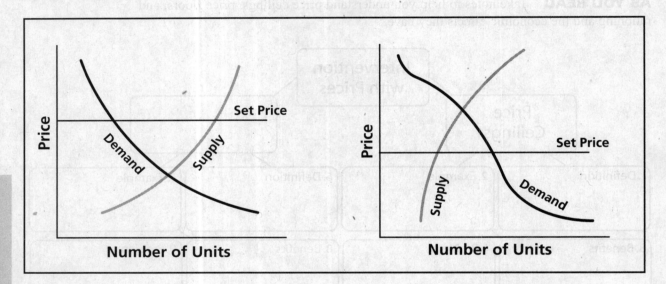

15. Reread your notes on price ceilings and price floors. Circle the point of market equilibrium on each graph. Note whether the set price is above or below market equilibrium.

16. Which graph shows the economic effects of rent control and which shows the economic effects of minimum-wage laws? Write a title above each graph that indicates your answer.

17. Based on the graphs, what would happen to the number of jobs in the low-wage job market if the government reduced the minimum wage?

_____

_____

18. Imagine a builder gets a grant to build low-income housing in the city. If the rent-control laws remained in effect, how would the graph change?

_____

_____

CHAPTER 6

SECTION 1

READING STUDY GUIDE
What Is Perfect Competition?

- **Before You Learned** There are many factors that affect supply and demand, which determine equilibrium market price.

- **Now You Will Learn** Perfect competition is the ideal by which economists measure all market structures.

AS YOU READ Take notes listing the characteristics of perfect competition. Use the cluster diagram on this page of the worksheet.

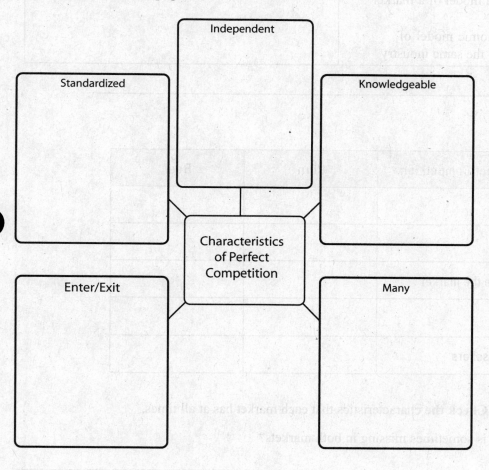

WHAT IS PERFECT COMPETITION?, *CONTINUED*

<table>
<tr><td>

VOCABULARY HUNT Write the letter of the term that best matches the description.

_____ 1. A business that accepts the market price determined by supply and demand

_____ 2. Occurs in markets with few sellers or products that are not alike

_____ 3. The ideal model of a market economy

_____ 4. An economic model of competition within the same industry

</td><td>

A. perfect competition

B. imperfect competition

C. market structure

D. price taker

</td></tr>
</table>

APPLICATION
Mark It Up!

Characteristic of Perfect Competition	Corn	Beef
Many buyers and sellers		
Standardized product		
Freedom to enter and leave the market		
Independent action		
Well-informed buyers and sellers		

5. Complete the chart. **Check the** characteristics that each market has at all times.

6. Which characteristic is sometimes missing in both markets?

_____

7. How does government affect competition in the corn market?

_____

_____

CHAPTER 7

Name _____ Date _____

READING STUDY GUIDE
The Impact of Monopoly

- **Before You Learned** Perfect competition is the most competitive market structure.

- **Now You Will Learn** A monopoly is the least competitive market structure.

AS YOU READ Take notes listing the characteristics of different types of monopolies. Use the chart below and on the next page of this worksheet.

	One Seller	Restricted Market	Control of Prices
Natural Monopoly			
Government Monopoly			
Technological Monopoly			
Geographic Monopoly			

VOCABULARY HUNT Circle each term where it appears in your notes and be sure you understand its meaning. If a term does not appear, write it in or next to the box where it best belongs.	monopoly price maker natural monopoly technological monopoly economies of scale	cartel barrier to entry government monopoly geographic monopoly patent

THE IMPACT OF MONOPOLY, *CONTINUED*

APPLICATION

Mark It Up!

© Clive Goddard/www.CartoonStock.com

13. Circle the word in the cartoon indicating that the cottage represents a monopoly.

14. Why are similar properties unlikely to be available?

_____

_____

_____

_____

15. What kind of monopoly does the cottage represent? Why?

_____

_____

_____

_____

CHAPTER 7

SECTION
3

READING STUDY GUIDE
Other Market Structures

- **Before You Learned** A monopoly is the least competitive market structure.
- **Now You Will Learn** Monopolistic competition and oligopoly fall between perfect competition and monopoly.

AS YOU READ Complete the chart on this worksheet to compare and contrast monopolistic competition and oligopoly.

Monopolistic Competition	Oligopoly

VOCABULARY HUNT Circle each term where it appears in your notes. If a term does not appear, write it in or next to the box where it best belongs. Then write the letter of the term next to the definition below which best describes it.

a. monopolistic competition

b. product differentiation

c. oligopoly

d. start-up costs

_____ 1. the effort to distinguish a product from similar products

_____ 2. market structure where only a few sellers offer similar but not identical products

_____ 3. occurs when many sellers offer similar products

_____ 4. expenses of a new business when it enters a market

CHAPTER 7

OTHER MARKET STRUCTURES, *CONTINUED*

APPLICATION

Mark It Up!

Market Structure	Number of Sellers	Type of Product	Sellers' Control over Prices	Barriers to Entry or Exit
Perfect Competition	Many / Few	Standardized	None	Many / Few
Monopolisitic Competition	Many / Few	Similar but differentiated	Limited	Many / Few
Oligopoly	Many / Few	Standardized for industry; differentiated for consumers	Some	Many / Few
Monopoly	One	Standardized, but no close substitutes	Significant	Very many

5. **Circle** the correct word—*many* or *few*—where both appear.

6. **How does monopolistic competition differ from perfect competition?**

_____

_____

_____

7. **Is an oligopoly more competitive or less competitive than a monopoly?**

_____

_____

SECTION
4

READING STUDY GUIDE
Regulation and Deregulation Today

- **Before You Learned** The U.S. economy uses government protections and regulations that alter the free enterprise system.

- **Now You Will Learn** Government uses regulation to promote competition and protect consumers.

AS YOU READ Take notes to keep track of main ideas and supporting details. Use the hierarchy diagram on this page of the worksheet. Fill in the top level of open areas with main ideas. Use the lower areas to add details.

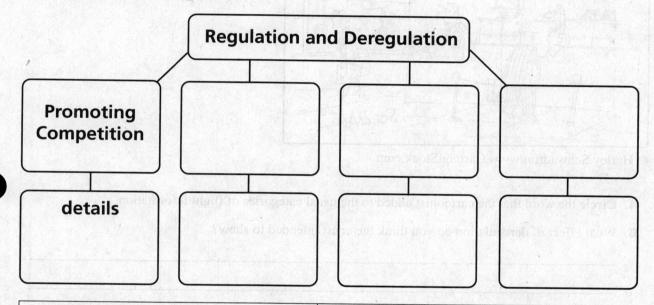

Regulation and Deregulation

Promoting Competition

details

VOCABULARY HUNT Circle each term where it appears in your notes and be sure you understand its meaning. If a term does not appear, write it in the box. Then fill in the term that best completes each of the following sentences.

1. If competing real estate agents agreed to divide up territory, it would be an example of _____.

2. _____ occurs when businesses agree to charge the same price for competing products.

3. The airlines industry has changed because of _____.

regulation	antitrust legislation
trust	merger
price fixing	market allocation
cease and desist order	public disclosure
deregulation	

CHAPTER 7

REGULATION AND DEREGULATION TODAY, *CONTINUED*

APPLICATION

Mark It Up!

© Harley Schwadron/www.CartoonStock.com

4. Circle the word that the cartoonist added to the usual categories of flight information.

5. What effect of deregulation do you think the artist intended to show?

_____

_____

6. Describe one positive effect of airline deregulation.

_____

_____

Economics: Concepts and Choices
Chapter 7: Market Structures

CHAPTER 7

SECTION
1

READING STUDY GUIDE
Sole Proprietorships

- **Before You Learned** Market structures vary from perfect competition to monopolies.

- **Now You Will Learn** The sole proprietorship is the most common type of business organization in the United States.

AS YOU READ   Take notes listing the advantages and disadvantages of sole proprietorships. Use the chart on this page of the worksheet. Use the diagram on the back of this worksheet to note how to start a sole proprietorship.

Sole Proprietorships	
Advantages	**Disadvantages**

VOCABULARY HUNT Circle each term where it appears in your notes and be sure you understand its meaning. If a term does not appear, write it in or next to the box where it best belongs.	business organization	limited life
	sole proprietorship	unlimited liability

CHAPTER 8

SOLE PROPRIETORSHIPS, *CONTINUED*

APPLICATION

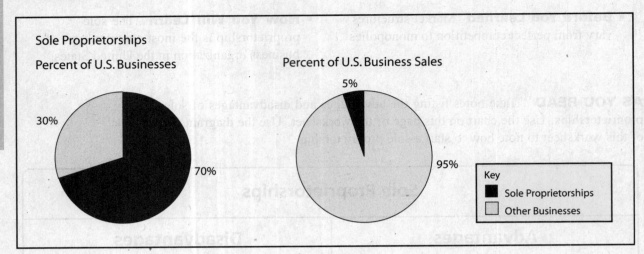

Sole Proprietorships
Percent of U.S. Businesses

30%

70%

Percent of U.S. Business Sales

5%

95%

Key
■ Sole Proprietorships
□ Other Businesses

1. **MARK IT UP!** The graph on the left shows the percent of U.S. businesses that are sole proprietorships. Circle that percentage on the graph.

2. According to the graph on the right, what percent of sales do sole proprietorships generate?

   _____

   _____

   _____

3. Write one reason why so many businesses generate such a small percentage of total sales.

   _____

   _____

SECTION 2

READING STUDY GUIDE

Forms of Partnerships

- **Before You Learned** A sole proprietorship is a type of business organization that has only one owner.

- **Now You Will Learn** A partnership is a type of business organization that has at least two owners.

AS YOU READ Compare and contrast sole proprietorships and partnerships. Take notes showing similarities and differences between them. Use the chart on this page of the worksheet.

Sole Proprietorship	Partnerships
One owner	Two or more owners

VOCABULARY HUNT Circle each term where it appears in your notes and be sure you understand its meaning. If a term does not appear, write it where it best belongs on one or both of the charts.	partnership limited liability partnership general partnership limited partnership

APPLICATION

Doe & Doe
Attorneys
at Law

1. **MARK IT UP!** Underline the names of the business owners.

2. Could this business register as a limited liability partnership? Explain your answer.

_____

_____

_____

3. Write what happens to a partnership when one partner dies.

_____

_____

SECTION

3

READING STUDY GUIDE

Corporations, Mergers, and Multinationals

- **Before You Learned** Sole proprietorships and partnerships are two types of business organizations.
- **Now You Will Learn** Corporations are another main type of business organization.

AS YOU READ Take notes that categorize information about corporations. Use the chart on this page of the worksheet.

Corporations	
Advantages	**Disadvantages**

VOCABULARY		
HUNT Circle each term where it appears in your notes and be sure you understand its meaning. If a term does not appear, write it in or next to the box where it best belongs.	corporation	public company
	stock	private company
	dividend	bond
	vertical merger	limited liability
	conglomerate	unlimited life
	multinational corporation	horizontal merger

CORPORATIONS, MERGERS, AND MULTINATIONALS, *CONTINUED*

APPLICATION

"I see there's been another merger."

© John Morris/CartoonStock.com

1. ***MARK IT UP!*** **Circle** the name of the merger.

2. Do you think that the merger is one likely to happen? Why or why not?

_____

_____

_____

3. Change the sign to reflect a different merger. Then write one reason why the merger
   you've chosen is likely to succeed.

_____

_____

SECTION
4

READING STUDY GUIDE
Franchises, Co-ops, and Nonprofits

- **Before You Learned** The purpose of most businesses is to make a profit.

- **Now You Will Learn** Cooperatives are business organizations that exist to provide goods or services to their members

AS YOU READ Take notes summarizing information on specialized organizations. Use the chart on this page.

Franchises	Co-Ops	Nonprofits

VOCABULARY HUNT Circle each term where it appears in your notes and be sure you understand its meaning. If a term does not appear, write it in or next to the box where it best belongs.	franchise franchisee	cooperative nonprofit organization

FRANCHISES, CO-OPS, AND NONPROFITS, *CONTINUED*

APPLICATION

Mark It Up!

1. **Circle** the word that identifies the co-op's members.

2. Which type of cooperative is Organic Valley most likely to be? Explain your answer.

   _____

   _____

   _____

3. **Write** two benefits for members of co-ops of the same type as Organic Valley.

   _____

   _____

   _____

   _____

Copyright © McDougal Littell/Houghton Mifflin Company.

SECTION 1

READING STUDY GUIDE

How Are Wages Determined?

- **Before You Learned** Supply and demand determine the market price for goods and services.

- **Now You Will Learn** Supply and demand determine how much a worker is paid.

AS YOU READ   Take notes on how wages are governed by supply and demand. Use the diagram on this worksheet.

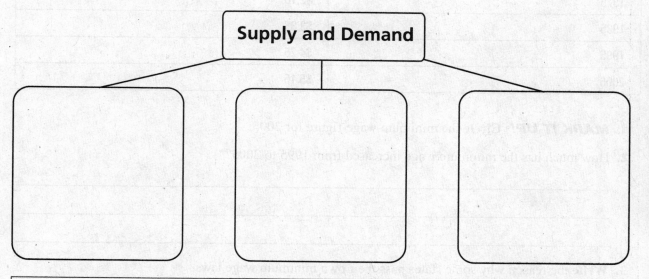

Supply and Demand

VOCABULARY HUNT Circle each term where it appears in your notes and be sure you understand its meaning. If a term does not appear, write it in or next to the box where it best belongs.

wages	equilibrium wage
derived demand	wage rate
human capital	minimum wage
glass ceiling	

CHAPTER 9

HOW ARE WAGES DETERMINED?, *CONTINUED*

APPLICATION

Federal Minimum Wage Rates, 1955–2005	
Year	Minimum Hourly Wage
1955	$0.75
1965	$1.25
1975	$2.10
1985	$3.35
1995	$4.25
2005	$5.15

1. **MARK IT UP!** Circle the minimum wage figure for 2005.

2. How much has the minimum wage increased from 1995 to 2005?

   _____

   _____

   _____

3. **Write** the reason why some states pass their own minimum wage laws.

   _____

   _____

CHAPTER 9

SECTION

2

READING STUDY GUIDE
Trends in Today's Labor Market

- **Before You Learned** Technology increases supply.

- **Now You Will Learn** Technology affects many jobs.

AS YOU READ   Take notes about the labor market. Use the diagram on this page of the worksheet. In each box, record main ideas about a trend.

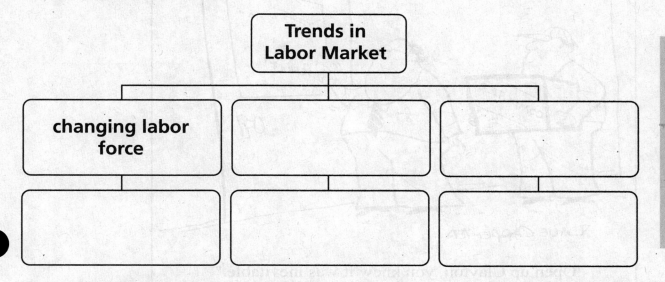

Trends in Labor Market

changing labor force

VOCABULARY HUNT Circle each term where it appears in your notes and be sure you understand its meaning. If a term does not appear, write it in or next to the box where it best belongs.

civilian labor force	outsourcing
insourcing	telecommuting
contingent employment	

TRENDS IN TODAY'S LABOR MARKET, *CONTINUED*

APPLICATION

"Open up Clayton, you knew it was inevitable."

© 2006 Dave Carpenter/www.CartoonStock.com

1. **MARK IT UP!** Circle the item representing a major change in the work force.

2. What basic skills are required by more and more jobs?

_____

_____

_____

3. **Write** one way that technology has changed the way people work.

_____

_____

SECTION 3 | READING STUDY GUIDE
Organized Labor in the United States

- **Before You Learned** Wages are the payments workers receive for work.

- **Now You Will Learn** Unions negotiate wage rates.

AS YOU READ Take notes summarizing the main ideas for each topic. Use the chart on both pages of the worksheet.

Topic	Main Ideas	Related Facts
Labor movement's rise to power		

VOCABULARY HUNT Circle each term where it appears in your notes and be sure you understand its meaning. If a term does not appear, write it in or next to the box where it best belongs.	labor union craft union closed shop right-to-work law bindng arbitration	strike industrial union union shop collective bargaining

CHAPTER 9

ORGANIZED LABOR IN THE UNITED STATES, *CONTINUED*

APPLICATION

Organized Labor in the United States

Before You Learned, Wages are the

As you read, Take notes summarizing the main idea on both pages in the worksheet.

Topic

Labor movement's rise to power

Vocabulary

where it appears in your table.

Craft union

industrial union

UNIONS:
They Brought
You The
8-Hour Day

1. *MARK IT UP!* **Underline** the benefit that unions obtained.

2. **Add** a second benefit to the poster.

3. **Write** two ways that unions resolve disagreements with management.

_____

_____

_____

_____

SECTION
1

READING STUDY GUIDE

Money: Its Functions and Properties

- **Before You Learned** A market is a place or situation in which people buy and sell goods and services.

- **Now You Will Learn** Money functions as a medium of exchange in the market.

AS YOU READ Take notes to summarize the key information about money. Use the cluster diagram on this page of the worksheet.

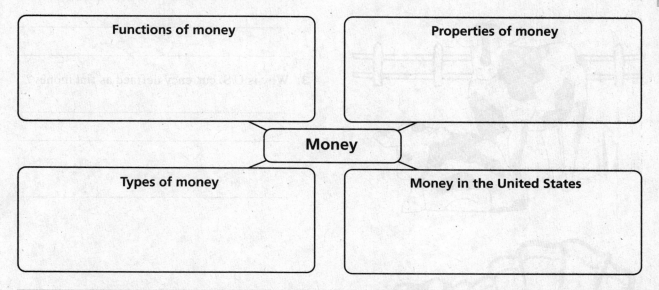

Functions of money		Properties of money
	Money	
Types of money		Money in the United States

VOCABULARY HUNT Circle each term where it appears in your notes and be sure you understand its meaning. If a term does not appear, write it in or next to the box where it best belongs.	money	medium of exchange
	barter	standard of value
	store of value	commodity money
	representative money	fiat money
	currency	demand deposits
	near money	

MONEY: ITS FUNCTIONS AND PROPERTIES, *CONTINUED*

APPLICATION

1. ***MARK IT UP!*** **Circle** the most portable form.

2. **Write** one reason why all three items have functioned as money.

_____

_____

_____

3. Why is U.S. currency defined as fiat money?

_____

_____

_____

_____

SECTION 2

READING STUDY GUIDE

The Development of U.S. Banking

- **Before You Learned** Money must have uniformity to be useful.

- **Now You Will Learn** The National Banking Act caused money to become uniform throughout the United States.

AS YOU READ Take notes listing key concepts and other helpful words and phrases. Use the chart on this page.

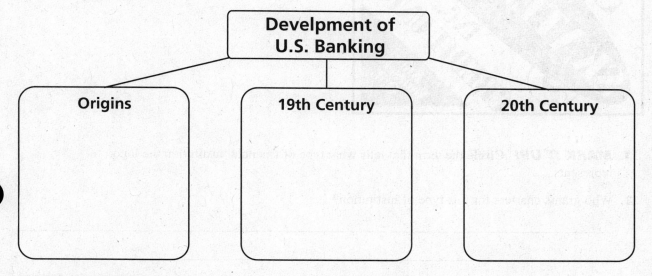

Develment of U.S. Banking

| Origins | 19th Century | 20th Century |

VOCABULARY HUNT Circle each term where it appears in your notes and be sure you understand its meaning. If a term does not appear, write it in or next to the box where it best belongs.

state bank   national bank
gold standard

CHAPTER 10

THE DEVELOPMENT OF U.S. BANKING, *CONTINUED*

APPLICATION

1. ***MARK IT UP!*** **Circle** the term that tells what type of financial institution the logo represents.

2. Who grants charters for this type of institution?

   _____

   _____

   _____

3. Write the main difference between this type of institution and other financial institutions.

   _____

   _____

SECTION 3

READING STUDY GUIDE

Innovations in Modern Banking

- **Before You Learned** The federal government played an important role in the development of U.S. banking.

- **Now You Will Learn** Deregulation has reduced government control of banking.

AS YOU READ Take notes to keep track of main ideas and supporting details. Use the following hierarchy diagram. Fill in the top row with main ideas. Use the bottom row to add details.

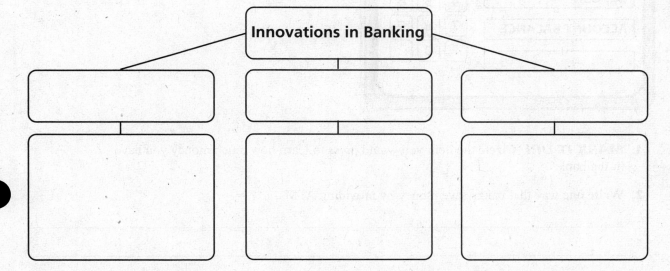

| VOCABULARY HUNT Circle each term where it appears in your notes and be sure you understand its meaning. If a term does not appear, write it in or next to the box where it best belongs. | automated teller machine   debit card
stored-value card |

INNOVATIONS IN MODERN BANKING, *CONTINUED*

APPLICATION

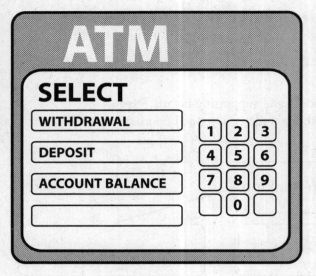

1. ***MARK IT UP!*** **Circle** the item you would press to learn how much money you have in the bank.

2. **Write** one way that banks save money by providing ATMs.

_____

_____

_____

3. **Write** one concern that some users have about electronic banking.

_____

_____

SECTION 1 | READING STUDY GUIDE
Savings and Investments

- **Before You Learned** Commercial banks, S&Ls, and credit unions take in deposits and provide loans.

- **Now You Will Learn** Commercial banks, S&Ls, and credit unions are financial intermediaries.

AS YOU READ Take notes to keep track of main ideas and supporting details. Use the hierarchy diagram on this worksheet. Fill in the top row with main ideas. Use the bottom row to add details.

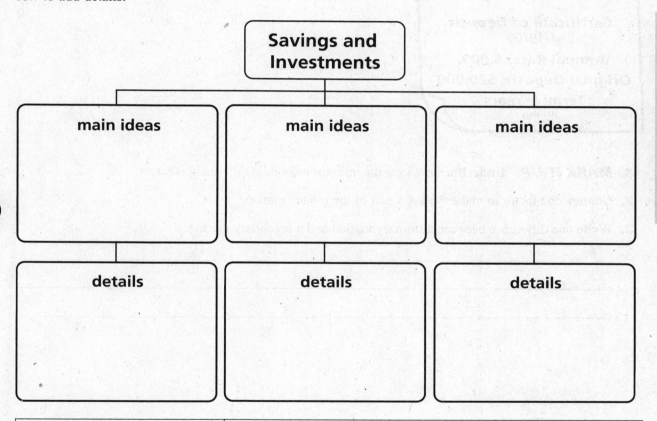

Savings and Investments

| main ideas | main ideas | main ideas |
| details | details | details |

CHAPTER 11

VOCABULARY HUNT Circle each term where it appears in your notes and be sure you understand its meaning. If a term does not appear, write it in or next to the box where it best belongs.

savings	investment
financial system	financial asset
financial market	financial intermediary
mutual fund	capital market
primary market	money market
secondary market	

SAVINGS AND INVESTMENTS, *CONTINUED*

APPLICATION

5 Year? CD

EVERYONE'S! BANK

Certificate of Deposit
4/19/00
Annual Rate: 6.00%
Original Deposit: $20,000
Term: 5 Years

1. *MARK IT UP!* **Underline** how long the investor must hold this financial asset.

2. **Change** one factor to make the asset part of the money market.

3. **Write** one difference between a primary market and a secondary market.

_____

_____

_____

SECTION 2

READING STUDY GUIDE
Investing in a Market Economy

- **Before You Learned** There are different types of financial assets.

- **Now You Will Learn** Several factors affect investment choices.

AS YOU READ Take notes listing key concepts and other useful words and phrases. Use the chart on this page of the worksheet.

Investing in a Market Economy	
objectives	**risk vs. return**

VOCABULARY HUNT Circle each term where it appears in your notes and be sure you understand its meaning. If a term does not appear, write it in or next to the box where it best belongs.	investment objective risk
	return diversification

CHAPTER 11

INVESTING IN A MARKET ECONOMY, *CONTINUED*

APPLICATION
MARK IT UP!

Gina's Notes on Investing

Goal: College tuition

Cash on hand: #1000

Years to Invest: 1 1/2

Source of Income:

coffee shop, 10 hrs/wk

Assets being considered:

• Shares of dot.com stock

• 18-month CD

1. **Underline** the lower-risk option.

2. **Circle** the option with the potential to make Gina more money.

3. **Write** one way that Gina could lose money if she chooses the 18-month CD.

_____

_____

CHAPTER 11

SECTION 3

READING STUDY GUIDE
Buying and Selling Stocks

- **Before You Learned** Corporations raise money by issuing stock and bonds.

- **Now You Will Learn** There are two types of stock, common and preferred.

AS YOU READ Take notes. Use the cluster diagram on this page of the worksheet to keep track of key concepts and other helpful words and phrases.

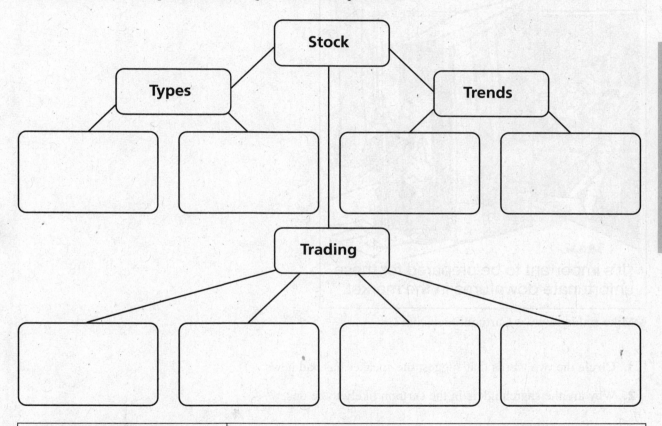

VOCABULARY HUNT
Circle each term where it appears in your notes and be sure you understand its meaning. If a term does not appear, write it in or next to the box where it best belongs.

stock exchange	capital gain
common stock	preferred stock
stockbroker	future
option	stock index
bull market	bear market

BUYING AND SELLING STOCKS, *CONTINUED*

APPLICATION
MARK IT UP!

© Mike Baldwin / Cornered

"It's important to be prepared for these unfortunate downturns in the market."

©Mike Baldwin/www.CartoonStock.com

1. Circle the two words that suggest the speaker has bad news.

2. Why are the shareholders in the cartoon likely to be upset?

_____

_____

_____

3. What usually causes an extended downturn?

_____

_____

Name ______________________________ Date ______________

SECTION 4

READING STUDY GUIDE

Bonds and Other Financial Instruments

- **Before You Learned** Corporations issue bonds.
- **Now You Will Learn** Governments may also issue bonds.

AS YOU READ Take notes to summarize information using key concepts and other helpful words and phrases. Use the chart on this page of the worksheet.

Bonds	Other Financial Instruments

VOCABULARY HUNT Circle each term where it appears in your notes and be sure you understand its meaning. If a term does not appear, write it in or next to the box where it best belongs.	par value coupon rate junk bond	maturity yield

CHAPTER 11

BONDS AND OTHER FINANCIAL INSTRUMENTS, *CONTINUED*

APPLICATION
MARK IT UP!

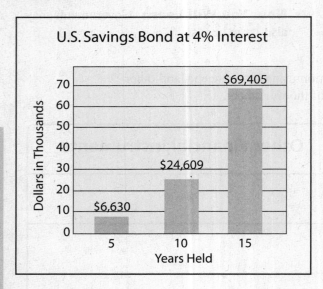

U.S. Savings Bond at 4% Interest

1. **Circle** the amount of return the investor would receive after holding the bond for 5 years.

2. **Draw** an arrow pointing to the amount an investor would receive after holding the bond for 15 years.

3. **Write** why U.S. savings bonds are considered to be low-risk.

   _____

   _____

   _____

Name _____   Date _____

SECTION
1

READING STUDY GUIDE
Gross Domestic Product and Other Indicators

- **Before You Learned** Macroeconomics looks at the economy as a whole.
- **Now You Will Learn** Macroeconomics analyzes the economy using national income accounting.

AS YOU READ Take notes to record what you learn about national income accounting. Use the diagram on this pages of the worksheet.

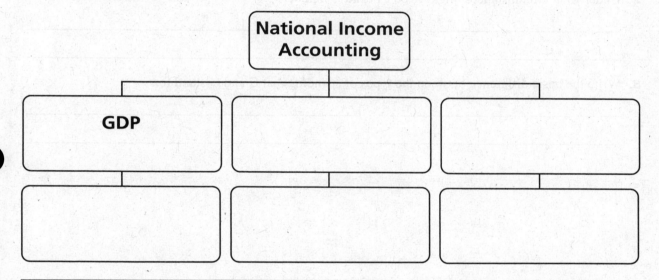

National Income Accounting

GDP

VOCABULARY HUNT Circle each term where it appears in your notes and be sure you understand its meaning. If a term does not appear, write it in or next to the box where it best belongs.

national income accounting	gross domestic product (GDP)
nominal GDP	real GDP
nonmarket activities	underground economy
gross national product (GNP)	net national product (NNP)
national income (NI)	personal income (PI)
disposable personal income (DPI)	

CHAPTER 12

GROSS DOMESTIC PRODUCT AND OTHER INDICATORS, *CONTINUED*

APPLICATION
Mark It Up!

$$C + I + G + X = GDP$$

1. Circle the letter that stands for spending by businesses.

2. Under what circumstances might X be a negative number?

   _____

   _____

3. Write the basic difference between the types of spending that C and G stand for.

   _____

   _____

SECTION
2 | READING STUDY GUIDE
Business Cycles

- **Before You Learned** GDP is used to evaluate a nation's economy.

- **Now You Will Learn** Changes in real GDP measure the business cycle.

AS YOU READ Take notes to record what you learn about business cycles. Use the cluster diagram on this page of the worksheet.

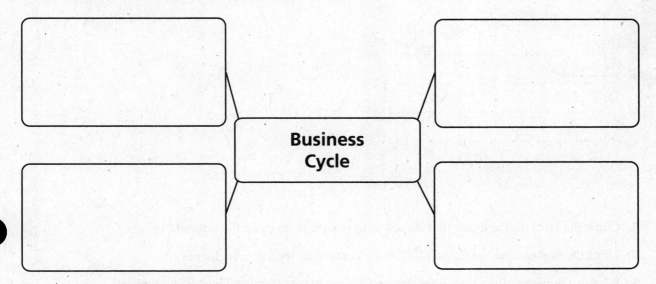

VOCABULARY HUNT Circle each term where it appears in your notes and be sure you understand its meaning. If a term does not appear, write it in or next to the box where it best belongs. Then write the term that best completes each sentence below.

1. Measures of economic performance that happen before changes in GDP are called _____.

2. A _____ is a contraction in the business cycle that continues for at least 6 months.

3. The worst _____ in U.S. history ended when the United States entered World War II.

4. Four stages make up the _____.

5. The total amount of goods and services that producers provide at each and every price level is called _____.

business cycle	economic growth
recession	depression
stagflation	aggregate demand
aggregate supply	macroeconomic equilibrium
leading indicators	coincident indicators
lagging indicators	

CHAPTER 12

BUSINESS CYCLES, *CONTINUED*

APPLICATION
Mark It Up!

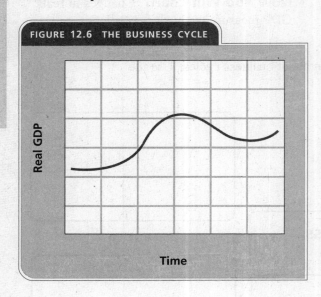

FIGURE 12.6   THE BUSINESS CYCLE

6. Circle the label on the graph that names what is used to measure the business cycle.

7. Label the highest and lowest portions of the curve with their correct names.

8. What is the name of the stage that occurs after the lowest stage and before the highest stage?

_____

SECTION

3

READING STUDY GUIDE

Stimulating Economic Growth

- **Before You Learned** Labor productivity is the amount of goods or services produced by a worker in an hour.
- **Now You Will Learn** Both capital and labor contribute to a nation's productivity.

AS YOU READ Take notes to summarize information on economic growth. Use the chart on this page of the worksheet.

What is Economic Growth?	What Determines Economic Growth?	Productivity and Economic Growth

VOCABULARY HUNT Circle each term where it appears in your notes and be sure you understand its meaning. If a term does not appear, write it in or next to the box where it best belongs. Then write the letter of the term next to the description below that best explains it.

1. _____ Enables workers to become more efficient
2. _____ Size of labor force X length of workweek
3. _____ Reflects efficiency
4. _____ Used to estimate a nation's economic growth

a. real GDP per capita   b. labor input

c. capital deepening   d. productivity

e. multifactor productivity

CHAPTER 12

STIMULATING ECONOMIC GROWTH, *CONTINUED*

APPLICATION
Mark It Up!

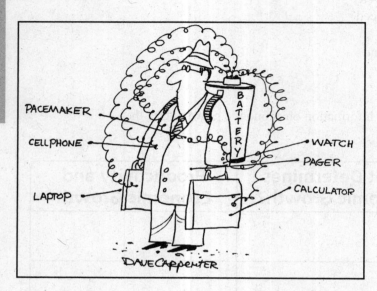

© Dave Carpenter/www.CartoonStock.com

5. Circle the item most representative of information technology.

6. How does technology contribute to economic growth?

_____

_____

7. In what way are computers in the workplace an example of capital deepening?

_____

_____

SECTION

1

READING STUDY GUIDE
Unemployment in Today's Economy

CHAPTER 13

- **Before You Learned** The civilian labor force is made up of people over the age of 16 who are employed or actively looking and available for work.

- **Now You Will Learn** The unemployment rate is the percentage of the labor force that is jobless and looking for work.

AS YOU READ Take notes to help you understand unemployment, how it is measured, and how it affects individuals and the economy.

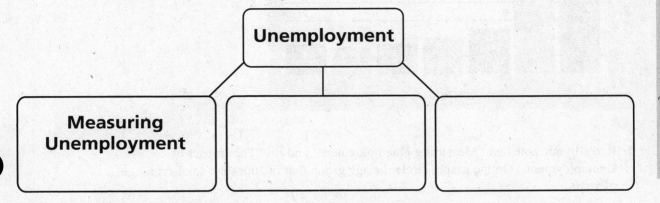

VOCABULARY HUNT		
Circle each term where it appears in your notes and be sure you understand its meaning. If a term does not appear, write it beside the box where it best belongs.	unemployment rate	frictional unemployment
	underemployed	structural unemployment
	ull employment	cyclical unemployment

UNEMPLOYMENT IN TODAY'S ECONOMY, *CONTINUED*

APPLICATION
Mark It Up!

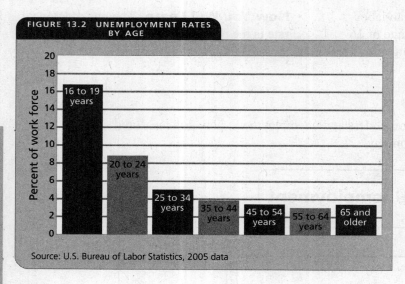

FIGURE 13.2 UNEMPLOYMENT RATES BY AGE

Percent of work force

16 to 19 years
20 to 24 years
25 to 34 years
35 to 44 years
45 to 54 years
55 to 64 years
65 and older

Source: U.S. Bureau of Labor Statistics, 2005 data

1. Reread your notes on "Measuring Unemployment" and on "The Impact of Unemployment." On the graph, circle the age group that includes the smallest range of years.

2. In which group was unemployment highest? In which group was unemployment the lowest?

   _____

   _____

3. Rank the groups from lowest to highest unemployment rate. Which effect of unemployment does this illustrate?

   _____

   _____

4. Why would unemployment rates be higher for younger age groups?

   _____

   _____

CHAPTER 13

SECTION

2

READING STUDY GUIDE

Poverty and Income Distribution

- **Before You Learned** The unemployment rate is the percentage of the labor force that is jobless and looking for work.

- **Now You Will Learn** Poverty is the situation in which a person's income and

resources do not allow him or her to achieve a minimum standard of living.

AS YOU READ Take notes to help you understand poverty, income distribution, and how they are interrelated.

What is Poverty?			

VOCABULARY HUNT Circle each term where it appears in your notes and be sure you understand its meaning. If a term does not appear, write it beside the box where it best belongs.	poverty threshold income distribution Lorenz curve	welfare workfare

POVERTY AND INCOME DISTRIBUTION, *CONTINUED*

APPLICATION
Mark It Up!

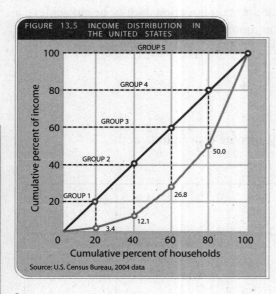

FIGURE 13.5 INCOME DISTRIBUTION IN THE UNITED STATES

GROUP 5

GROUP 4

GROUP 3

GROUP 2

GROUP 1

50.0

26.8

12.1

3.4

Cumulative percent of income

Cumulative percent of households

Source: U.S. Census Bureau, 2004 data

1. Reread your notes on "Income Distribution." Underline the type of graph that shows income distribution. On the graph shown here, indicate the graph type and draw an arrow pointing to the part that shows an equal distribution of income.

2. According to this graph, how much of the total income of the United States does the top 20 percent of all households receive?

_____

3. If income were distributed more equally, which of the five groups would gain a larger share of cumulative income? What would happen to the group or groups that did not gain more?

_____

_____

_____

4. If income were distributed more equally, what would happen to the curve and the diagonal line?

_____

_____

Economics: Concepts and Choices
Chapter 13: Facing Economic Challenges

CHAPTER 13

SECTION
3

READING STUDY GUIDE

Causes and Consequences of Inflation

- **Before You Learned** Poverty is the situation in which a person's income and resources do not allow him or her to achieve a minimum standard of living

- **Now You Will Learn** Inflation is a sustained rise in the general price level, which has negative effects on the economy and on economic stability.

AS YOU READ Take notes to help you understand inflation and its effects.

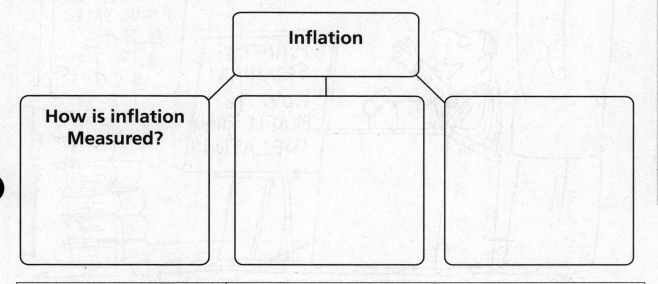

Inflation

How is inflation Measured?

VOCABULARY *HUNT* Circle each term where it appears in your notes and be sure you understand its meaning. If the term does not appear, reread the section and add the term and information about the term to your notes.	inflation deflation	demand-pull inflation cost-push inflation

CAUSES AND CONSEQUENCES OF INFLATION, *CONTINUED*

APPLICATION
Mark It Up!

© Harley Schwadron/www.CartoonStock.com

1. Reread your notes related to inflation and highlight the definition of the term. Circle the words in the cartoon that describe what people hope to learn at this seminar.

2. What happened to the price of the book being sold at the seminar?

_____

_____

3. Describe the cartoonist's use of ironic humor.

_____

_____

SECTION
1 READING STUDY GUIDE
How Taxes Work

CHAPTER 14

- **Before You Learned** Unemployment, poverty, and inflation all affect the economy in negative ways.

- **Now You Will Learn** The government raises money to provide public goods mainly by collecting taxes.

AS YOU READ Take notes to help you understand principles and criteria for taxation, tax bases, tax structures, and who pays taxes.

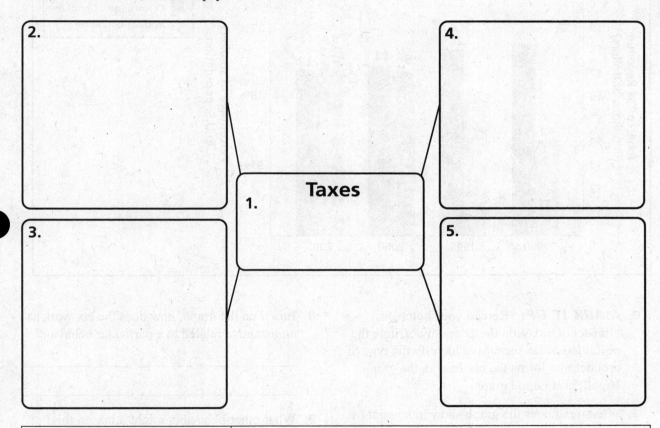

2.

4.

1. **Taxes**

3.

5.

VOCABULARY HUNT
Circle each term where it appears in your notes and be sure you understand its meaning. If a term does not appear, write it beside the box where it best belongs.

tax base	regressive tax
proportional tax	tax incentive
progressive tax	

CHAPTER 14

HOW TAXES WORK, *CONTINUED*

APPLICATION

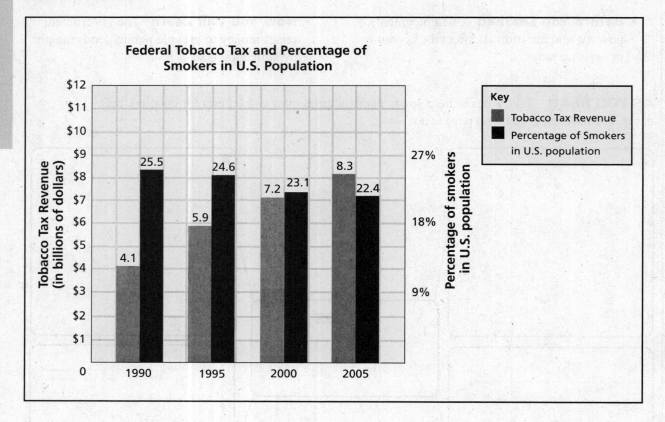

Federal Tobacco Tax and Percentage of Smokers in U.S. Population

Key
- Tobacco Tax Revenue
- Percentage of Smokers in U.S. population

6. **MARK IT UP!** Reread your notes on "Impact of Taxes on the Economy." Circle the definition of tax incentive. Identify the type of product that forms the tax base in the graph. Highlight it on the graph.

7. What trend does the graph show in amount of revenue the government collected from the tax over time? What trend does the graph show related to the percent of smokers in the U.S. population?

_____

_____

_____

8. Based on the graph, how does the tax work as an incentive related to a particular behavior?

_____

_____

9. What other behaviors might a tax on this product affect? Explain.

_____

_____

SECTION
2 | READING STUDY GUIDE
Federal Taxes

- **Before You Learned** The government raises money to provide public goods mainly by collecting taxes.
- **Now You Will Learn** The federal government raises money by levying the

following taxes: individual income tax, FICA taxes, corporate income tax, and several other minor taxes.

AS YOU READ   Take notes to help you understand the different taxes that the federal government levies.

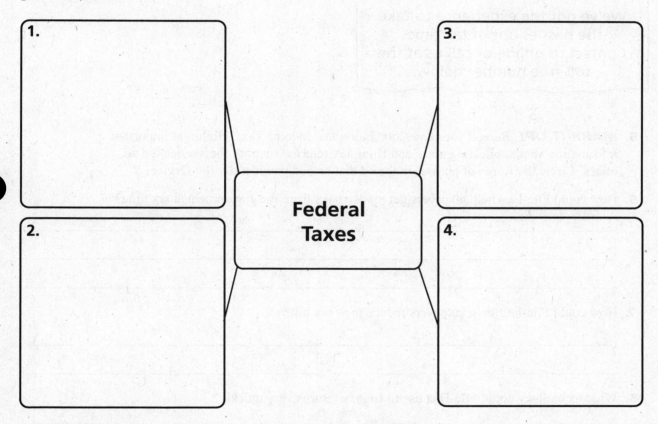

VOCABULARY HUNT Circle each term where it appears in your notes and be sure you understand its meaning. If a term does not appear, write it beside the box where it best belongs.	withholding	FICA
	taxable income	tax return

FEDERAL TAXES, *CONTINUED*

CHAPTER 14

APPLICATION

If you are like millions of other taxpayers, the government owes you money.
File-Fast Tax Services can help you get your money back FAST!

FILE-FAST TAX SERVICES

We've got the experience to take the hassles out of tax time.
Contact us online or call us at the toll-free number below.

5. **MARK IT UP!** Reread your notes on "Individual Income Tax." Highlight important information about collecting taxes and filing tax returns. Identify the service the ad offers. Circle the words of phrases in the ad that helped you identify the service.

6. How could File-Fast help taxpayers get money back from the government at tax time?

_____

_____

_____

7. How could File-Fast help taxpayers reduce their tax bill?

_____

_____

8. What technology could File-Fast use to file tax returns very quickly?

_____

_____

SECTION 3

READING STUDY GUIDE

Federal Government Spending

- **Before You Learned** he federal government raises money by levying the following taxes: individual income tax, FICA taxes, corporate income tax, and several other minor taxes.

- **Now You Will Learn** The federal government spends money on mandatory programs, such as Social Security, which are required by current law, and discretionary programs, for which spending is authorized each year.

AS YOU READ Take notes to help you understand how federal spending is authorized and budgeted and how federal government payments are made.

Federal Spending

1.

2.

3.

4.

5.

6.

VOCABULARY HUNT
Circle each term where it appears in your notes and be sure you understand its meaning. If a term does not appear, write it beside the box where it best belongs.

mandatory spending	appropriations
discretionary spending	grant-in-aid

Economics: Concepts and Choices
Chapter 14: Government Revenue and Spending

FEDERAL GOVERNMENT SPENDING, *CONTINUED*

APPLICATION

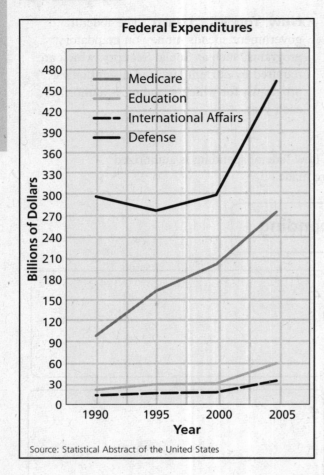

Federal Expenditures

Billions of Dollars

480
450
420
390
360
330
300
270
240
210
180
150
120
90
60
30
0

Medicare
Education
International Affairs
Defense

1990   1995   2000   2005

Year

Source: Statistical Abstract of the United States

7. *MARK IT UP!* Reread your notes on "Federal Expenditures." Circle the programs for which federal spending is mandatory. Underline the programs for which spending is discretionary. Do the same with the programs listed in the key of the graph.

8. Which program had the highest overall spending over the period the graph covers? Which program had the steepest increase overall during the period the graph covers?

_____

_____

_____

9. What trend does the graph show in federal expenditures for these programs?

_____

_____

10. Describe any exceptions you notice to the general trend.

_____

_____

11. Could the changes in government spending for these programs be due solely to economic changes, such as inflation or deflation? Explain your answer.

_____

_____

SECTION
4

READING STUDY GUIDE

State and Local Taxes and Spending

- **Before You Learned** The federal government spends money on mandatory programs, such as Social Security, which are required by current law, and discretionary programs, for which spending is authorized each year.

- **Now You Will Learn** State and local governments raise revenues from a variety of sources and spend the revenues on a variety of public goods.

AS YOU READ Take notes to help you understand how state and local governments raise and spend money.

State Government		Local Government	
Revenue	**Spending**	**Revenue**	**Spending**
1.	2.	3.	4.

VOCABULARY HUNT Circle each term where it appears in your notes and be sure you understand its meaning. If a term does not appear, write it beside the box where it best belongs.	balanced budget operating budge	capital budget tax assessor

STATE AND LOCAL TAXES AND SPENDING, *CONTINUED*

APPLICATION

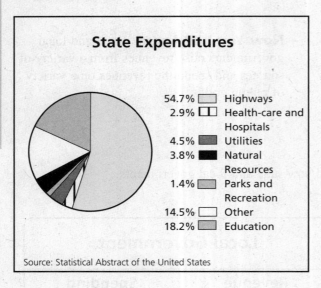

State Expenditures

54.7%	Highways
2.9%	Health-care and Hospitals
4.5%	Utilities
3.8%	Natural Resources
1.4%	Parks and Recreation
14.5%	Other
18.2%	Education

Source: Statistical Abstract of the United States

5. *MARK IT UP!* Reread your notes on "State Budgets and Spending." Highlight the programs listed that states spend money on. On the graph, circle the types of programs listed in your notes that are also on the graph.

6. Which type of program formed the largest part of state budgets in 2001?

_____

_____

7. Based on the discussion of state expenses in the section, what are four other expenses probably included in the "Other" category of the graph?

_____

_____

8. Do you think this graph is likely to include spending related to states' capital budgets? Why or why not?

_____

_____

Name _____ **Date** _____

SECTION

1

READING STUDY GUIDE

What Is Fiscal Policy?

- **Before You Learned** The federal government affects the nation's economy by influencing resource allocation, redistributing income, and competing with the private sector in a few industries

- **Now You Will Learn** The federal government uses fiscal policy tools, including taxation and spending, to affect the economy in deliberate ways.

AS YOU READ Take notes to help you understand fiscal policy, its purposes, and its limitations.

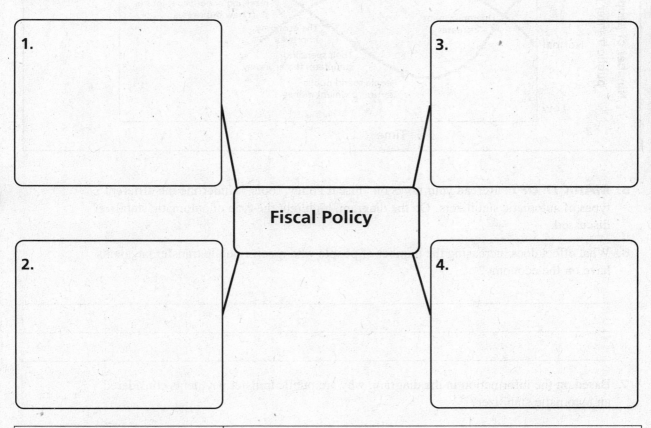

1.

2.

3.

4.

Fiscal Policy

VOCABULARY HUNT Circle each term where it appears in your notes and be sure you understand its meaning. If a term does not appear, write it beside the box where it best belongs.	expansionary fiscal policy	discretionary fiscal policy
	contractionary fiscal policy	automatic stabilizer

WHAT IS FISCAL POLICY?, *CONTINUED*

APPLICATION

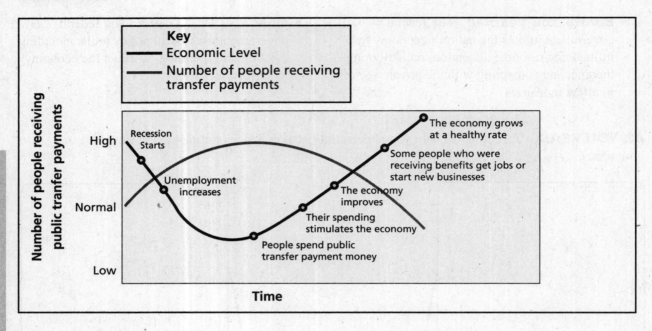

5. **MARK IT UP!**   Reread your notes on "Fiscal Policy Tools." Underline the different types of automatic stabilizers. On the diagram, highlight the type of automatic stabilizer discussed.

6. What effect does increasing the number of people who receive public transfer payments have on the economy?

   _____

   _____

   _____

7. Based on the information in the diagram, why are public transfer payments considered an automatic stabilizer?

   _____

   _____

8. How might the economic level change if the government implemented an expansionary fiscal policy at the point when the economy started to improve? Refer to the diagram in your answer.

   _____

   _____

Name _____ Date _____

READING STUDY GUIDE
Demand-Side and Supply-Side Policies

- **Before You Learned** The federal government uses fiscal policy tools, including taxation and spending, to affect the economy in deliberate ways.

- **Now You Will Learn** Demand-side and supply-side policies each can be used to try to stimulate the economy.

AS YOU READ Take notes to help you understand and evaluate demand-side and supply-side economic policies.

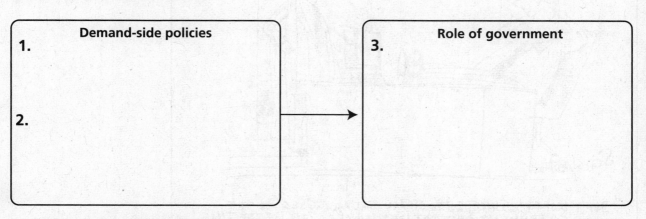

Demand-side policies

1.

2.

Role of government

3.

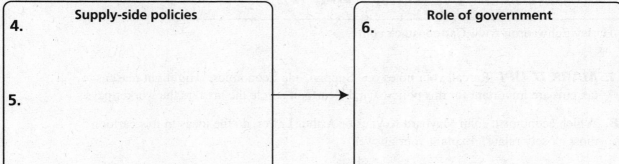

Supply-side policies

4.

5.

Role of government

6.

VOCABULARY HUNT Circle each term where it appears in your notes and be sure you understand its meaning. If a term does not appear, reread the section and add information about the term to your notes.

Keynsian economics	supply-side fiscal policy
demand-side fiscal policy	Laffer Curve
spending multiplier effect	

DEMAND-SIDE AND SUPPLY-SIDE POLICIES, *CONTINUED*

APPLICATION

© Harley Schwadron/www.Cartoonstock.com

7. **MARK IT UP!** Reread your notes on "Supply-Side Economics." Highlight reasons tax cuts are important for this policy. On the cartoon, circle the tax rate the worker pays.

8. Which economist, John Maynard Keynes or Arthur Laffer, do the ideas in this cartoon most closely relate? Explain your answer.

_____

9. Based on what you've read in this chapter, how does the tax rate mentioned in the caption compare with those from the 1970s? Based on the caption, what generalization can you make related to how taxpayers feel about any tax rate?

_____

10. Which type of tax is the character in the cartoon referring to? (Hint: Refer to Chapter 14.) What other taxes would the character also be likely to have to pay? Based on this information, how would you change the caption?

_____

SECTION
3
READING STUDY GUIDE
Deficits and the National Debt

- **Before You Learned** Demand-side and supply-side policies each can be used to try to stimulate the economy.
- **Now You Will Learn** Deficit spending has caused the United States to run up a large national debt, which affects the health of the economy.

AS YOU READ   Take notes to help you understand the national budget, deficit spending, and the national debt and how the national debt affects the economy.

Federal Deficits	National Debt
1.	4.
2.	5.
3.	6.

VOCABULARY HUNT Circle each term where it appears in your notes and be sure you understand its meaning. If a term does not appear, write it beside the box where it best belongs.	deficit spending national debt	trust funds crowding-out effect

CHAPTER 15

DEFICITS AND THE NATIONAL DEBT, *CONTINUED*

APPLICATION

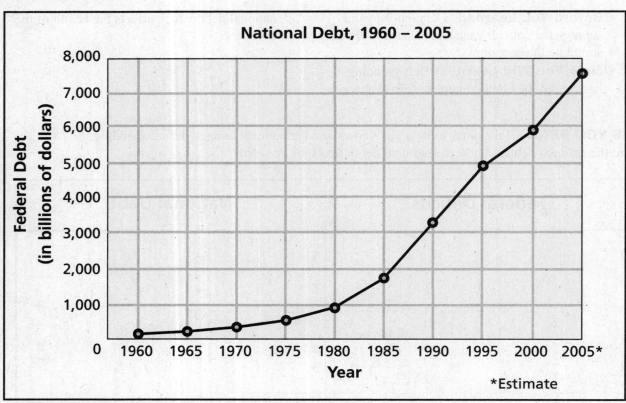

National Debt, 1960 – 2005

Source: *Statistical Abstract of the United States*

7. **MARK IT UP!** Reread your notes on "The Federal Deficit and Debt." Underline definitions of budget surplus, budget deficit, deficit spending, and national debt On the graph, circle the main topic. Highlight the units it is measured in.

8. circle the decade in which the graph shows the steepest rise: 1960s, 1970s, 1980s, 1990s.

9. Circle the period when the graph shows a less steep rise: 1980-1985; 1985-1990; 1990-1995; 1995-2000; 2000-2005.

_____

_____

10. How does the graph on textbook page 463 help explain the answer to question 25?

_____

_____

11. How does the trend the graph shows relate to deficit spending and debt servicing?

_____

_____

CHAPTER 15

SECTION 1

READING STUDY GUIDE
The Federal Reserve System

- **Before You Learned** Opposition to the First and Second Banks of the United States caused economic instability.

- **Now You Will Learn** In 1913 Congress established the Federal Reserve System, a true central bank.

AS YOU READ Take notes to identify the major characteristics of the Federal Reserve System. Use the diagram on this page of the worksheet.

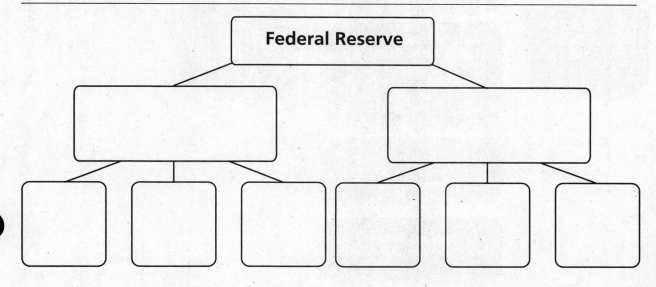

VOCABULARY HUNT Circle each term where it appears in your notes and be sure understand its meaning. If a term does not appear, write it in or next to the box where it best belongs.	central bank	monetary
	Federal Reserve System	currency
	Board of Governors	thrift institution
	Federal Open Market Committee	

CHAPTER 16

THE FEDERAL RESERVE SYSTEM, *CONTINUED*

APPLICATION
Mark It Up!

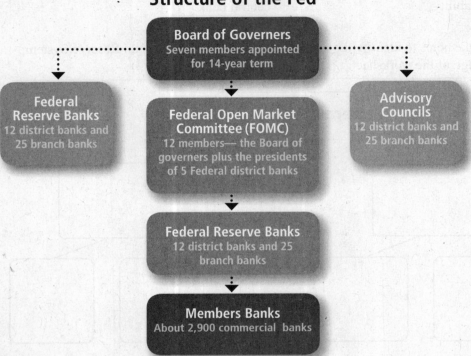

Structure of the Fed

Board of Governers
Seven members appointed
for 14-year term

**Federal
Reserve Banks**
12 district banks and
25 branch banks

**Federal Open Market
Committee (FOMC)**
12 members— the Board of
governers plus the presidents
of 5 Federal district banks

**Advisory
Councils**
12 district banks and
25 branch banks

Federal Reserve Banks
12 district banks and 25
branch banks

Members Banks
About 2,900 commercial banks

1. Which group oversees the operations of the Fed?

_____

2. Into how many districts is the Fed organized?

_____

3. Explain how the structure of the Fed ensures that the interests of all regions of the
country and all sectors of the economy are represented.

_____

_____

_____

CHAPTER 16

SECTION
2

READING STUDY GUIDE
Functions of the Federal Reserve

- **Before You Learned** The federal government receives money from taxes that it spends on a variety of programs.

- **Now You Will Learn** The Fed helps the government carry out its spending activities.

AS YOU READ Take notes to identify the major functions of the Federal Reserve. Use the chart on this page of the worksheet.

Functions of the Federal Reserve		
Serving the banking system	**Serving the federal government**	**Creating money**

VOCABULARY HUNT Circle each term where it appears in your notes and be sure you understand its meaning. If a term does not appear, write it in or next to the box where it best belongs.

check clearing

bank exams

deposit multiplier formula

bank holding company

required reserve ratio

CHAPTER 16

FUNCTIONS OF THE FEDERAL RESERVE, *CONTINUED*

APPLICATION

◄ BACK ► FORWARD ‖ STOP ↻ REFRESH ⌂ HOME   ☒

NEWS.COM
WORLD | US | BUSINESS | SCI/TECH | SPORTS | ENTERTAINMENT | HEALTH

Oil Prices Rise Sharply
Transportation costs up

1. **MARK IT UP!** How would the situation in the headline affect the demand for money? Explain your answer.

_____

_____

_____

2. Would the Fed be more likely to increase or decrease the money supply?

_____

_____

_____

3. How would the RRR probably change? Explain your answer.

_____

_____

_____

CHAPTER 16

SECTION
3

READING STUDY GUIDE
Monetary Policy

- **Before You Learned** Fiscal policy is the federal government's use of taxes and spending to affect the economy.

- **Now You Will Learn** Monetary policy is actions of the Federal Reserve to affect the economy by changing the money supply.

AS YOU READ Take notes to track main ideas and supporting details on monetary policy. Use the diagram on this page of the worksheet.

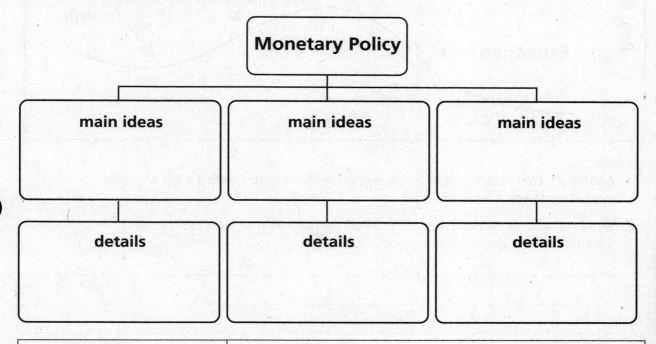

Monetary Policy

main ideas	main ideas	main ideas
details	details	details

MARK IT UP! Circle each term where it appears in your notes and be sure you understand its meaning. If a term does not appear, write it in or next to the box where it best belongs.	Monetary policy Discount rate Prime rate Open market operations Federal funds rate	Expansionary monetary policy Easy-money policy Contractionary monetary policy Tight-money policy Monetarism

CHAPTER 16

MONETARY POLICY, *CONTINUED*

APPLICATION

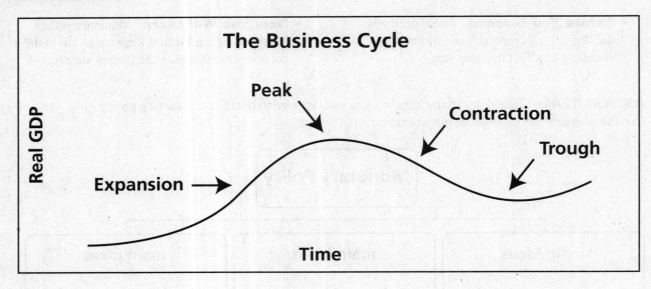

The Business Cycle

1. **MARK IT UP!** Mark an X at the stage of the business cycle where the Fed would be most likely to buy bonds.

2. Write the stage of the business cycle at which the Fed would be most likely to raise the discount rate. Explain your answer.

   _____

   _____

   _____

3. Circle the stage at which the Fed would be most likely to apply an expansionary monetary policy. Explain your answer.

   _____

   _____

   _____

CHAPTER 16

SECTION

4

READING STUDY GUIDE

Applying Monetary and Fiscal Policy

- **Before You Learned** Fiscal and monetary policies use different tools to stabilize the economy.

- **Now You Will Learn** Fiscal and monetary policies can affect each other.

AS YOU READ Use the cause-and-effect chart below to note key concepts and other helpful words and phrases.

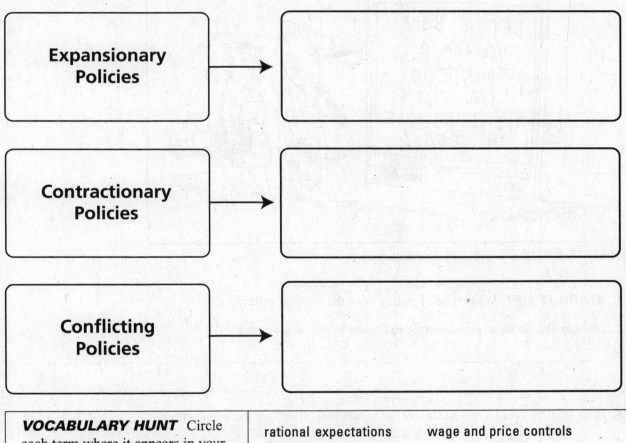

Expansionary Policies	→	
Contractionary Policies	→	
Conflicting Policies	→	

VOCABULARY HUNT Circle each term where it appears in your notes and be sure you understand its meaning. If a term does not appear, write it in or next to the box where it best belongs.

rational expectations theory   wage and price controls

CHAPTER 16

APPLYING MONETARY AND FISCAL POLICY, *CONTINUED*

APPLICATION

© Harley Schwadron/www.CartoonStock.com

1. **MARK IT UP!** What type of policy does the cartoon reflect?

2. Identify the name of an economic tool used by the government.

_____

_____

3. How might buying a trip to Las Vegas would help stimulate the economy.

_____

_____

_____

SECTION
1

READING STUDY GUIDE
Benefits and Issues of International Trade

- **Before You Learned** Supply and demand interact to determine equilibrium price.

- **Now You Will Learn** Exports and imports affect supply and demand.

AS YOU READ Use the diagram on this page of the worksheet to note key concepts and other helpful words and phrases.

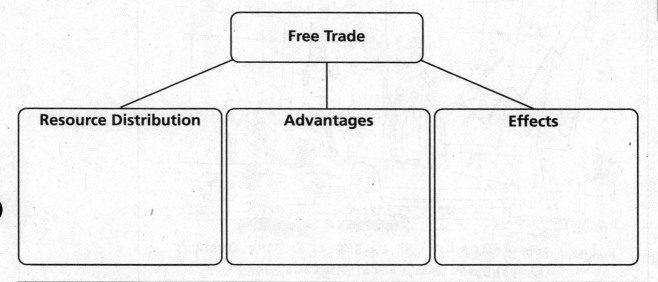

Free Trade

Resource Distribution

Advantages

Effects

VOCABULARY HUNT Circle each term where it appears in your notes and be sure you understand its meaning. If a term does not appear, write it in or next to the box where it best belongs. Then complete the cause and effect chart below. Write the appropriate term in each empty space.

specialization

absolute advantage

law of comparative advantage

imports

economic interdependence

comparative advantage

exports

BENEFITS AND ISSUES OF INTERNATIONAL TRADE, *CONTINUED*

APPLICATION
Mark It Up!

© Harley Schwadron/www.CartoonStock.com

1. What effect has foreign competition had on the profits of the company shown?

   _____

   _____

2. How does competition from foreign imports affect supply?

   _____

   _____

3. Write one way that consumers benefit from increased competition.

   _____

   _____

SECTION
2

READING STUDY GUIDE
Trade Barriers

- **Before You Learned** International trade affects prices and quantity.

- **Now You Will Learn** Trade barriers limit trade between nations.

AS YOU READ Take notes listing barriers to trade. Use the cause-and-effect chart on this page of the worksheet.

Cause	Effect
	Hurts domestic producers
	Raises prices on imports
	Limits exports
	Cuts off trade with another country

VOCABULARY HUNT Circle each term where it appears in your notes and be sure you understand its meaning. If a term does not appear, write it in or next to the box where it best belongs.	trade barrier tariff embargo revenue tariffs trade war protectionism	quota voluntary export restraint dumping protective tariffs protectionism

TRADE BARRIERS, *CONTINUED*

APPLICATION
Mark It Up!

Miami Tribune

August 30, 2006

Cubans Rely on old U.S. cars

---

1. Which type of trade barrier led to the headline?

_____

2. How might the U.S. decision to stop trading with Cuba have affected the American auto industry?

_____

3. How might stopping trade with Cuba have affected Cuban exports?

_____

SECTION 3

READING STUDY GUIDE
Measuring the Value of Trade

- **Before You Learned** Imports and exports affect prices and quantity.

- **Now You Will Learn** Imports and exports determine a nation's balance of trade.

AS YOU READ Take notes. Use the cluster diagram on this page of the worksheet to record key concepts, as well as other helpful words and phrases.

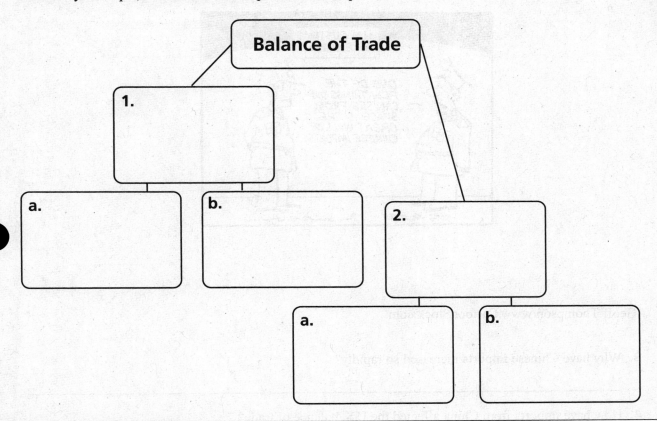

Balance of Trade

1.

a.

b.

2.

a.

b.

VOCABULARY HUNT Circle each term where it appears in your notes and be sure you understand its meaning. If a term does not appear, write it in or next to the box where it best belongs.

foreign exchange market	foreign exchange rate
fixed rate of exchange	flexible rate of exchange
trade weighted value of the dollar	balance of trade
balance of payments	trade surplus
trade deficit	

CHAPTER 17

MEASURING THE VALUE OF TRADE, *CONTINUED*

APPLICATION

Mark It Up!

© Geoff Thompson/www.CartoonStock.com

3. Why have Chinese imports increased so rapidly?

_____

4. How have imports from China affected the U.S. balance of trade?

_____

5. Write one reason for the U.S. having become the number one destination for Chinese
exports.

_____

SECTION
4

READING STUDY GUIDE
Modern International Institutions

- **Before You Learned** Nations trade in a world market.

- **Now You Will Learn** Nations organize regional trading groups.

AS YOU READ Take notes to summarize the section. Use the chart on this page of the worksheet.

Regional	International

VOCABULARY HUNT Circle each term where it appears in your notes and be sure you understand its meaning. If a term does not appear, write it in or next to the box where it best belongs. Then write the letter of the term on the line before the description below that bests defines it

_____ 1. Organized to control oil

_____ 2. Calls for a phase-out of trade barriers between Canada, Mexico, the United States

_____ 3. Oversees and encourages international trade

_____ 4. Agreement that abolishes trade barriers among member nations

_____ 5. Union of nations that has a common currency

a. EU

b. euro

c. NAFTA

d. OPEC

e. cartel

f. WTO

g. free trade zone

h. customs union

MODERN INTERNATIONAL INSTITUTIONS, *CONTINUED*

APPLICATION

Mark It Up!

U.S. Balance of Trade with the EU (in millions of dollars)			
Year	Exports	Imports	Balance
1990	98,128.9	91,876.8	6,252.10
1995	123,671.1	131,870.8	−8,199.70
2000	165,064.5	220,018.6	−54,954.10
2005	181,718.3	298,878.5	−117,160.30

Source: U.S. Census Bureau

6. In what year did the United States have the most favorable balance of trade with the EU15? The least favorable?

_____

7. What trend can be seen in the balance of trade from 1990 to 2005?

_____

_____

_____

8. Using this chart, what predictions could you make about 2010?

_____

_____

_____

READING STUDY GUIDE
Definitions of Development

- **Before You Learned** Economists use GDP to analyze a nation's economy.
- **Now You Will Learn** Economists use GDP per capita to define a nation's level of economic development.

AS YOU READ Take notes listing levels and measures of development. Use the chart on this page of the worksheet.

Standards	Measures
Health	
Consumption	
Education	
Energy Use	
Labor	

VOCABULARY HUNT Circle each term where it appears in your notes and be sure you understand its meaning. If a term does not appear, write it in or next to the box where it best belongs. Then find the term that best matches each definition below. Write the letter of the term on the line provided.

_____ 1. Percentage of a population that can read and write

_____ 2. Countries that move from a command economy to a market economy

_____ 3. Systems that support an economy

_____ 4. Average amount of goods and services produced by one person

_____ 5. Nations with a high standard of living

a. developed nations

b. less developed countries

c. infrastructure

d. transitional economies

e. per capita GDP

f. infant mortality rate

g. life expectancy

h. literacy rate

DEFINITIONS OF DEVELOPMENT, *CONTINUED*

APPLICATION

Mark It Up!

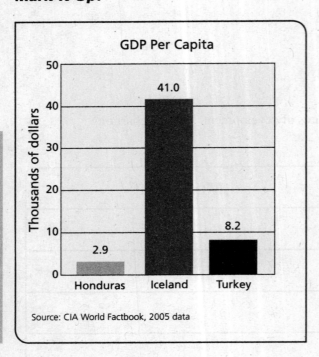

GDP Per Capita

Thousands of dollars

- Honduras — 2.9
- Iceland — 41.0
- Turkey — 8.2

Source: CIA World Factbook, 2005 data

6. What economic factor does GDP per capita estimate?

_____

7. **Circle** the name of the country most likely to have the highest standard of living.

8. **Which** country is most likely to have an industrial economy? Explain your answer.

_____

_____

SECTION 2

READING STUDY GUIDE

A Framework for Economic Development Objectives

- **Before You Learned** Human capital is the knowledge and skills that enable workers to be productive.

- **Now You Will Learn** Investment in human capital is important to developing economies.

AS YOU READ Take notes using the key concepts and other helpful words and phrases. Use the cluster diagram below.

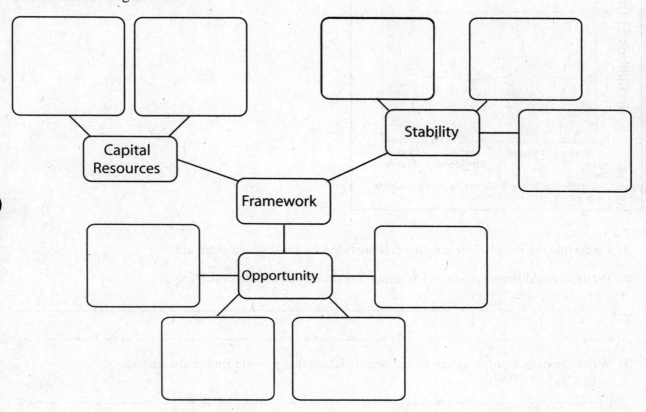

VOCABULARY HUNT Circle each term where it appears in your notes and be sure you understand its meaning. If a term does not appear, write it in or next to the box where it best belongs.

external debt

World Bank

debt restructuring

United Nations Development Program (UNDP)

default

International Monetary Fund (IMF)

stabilization program

CHAPTER 18

A FRAMEWORK FOR ECONOMIC DEVELOPMENT OBJECTIVES, *CONTINUED*

APPLICATION

Mark It Up!

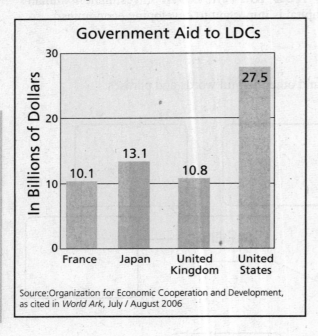

Government Aid to LDCs

In Billions of Dollars

France	10.1
Japan	13.1
United Kingdom	10.8
United States	27.5

Source: Organization for Economic Cooperation and Development, as cited in *World Ark*, July / August 2006

1. Underline the name of the country that provided the most government aid.

2. Write two additional means of financing less developed countries (LDCs).

_____

_____

3. Write the names of two international organizations that provide financial assistance to LDCs.

_____

_____

CHAPTER 18

SECTION
3

READING STUDY GUIDE
Economic Development Objectives

- **Before You Learned** Transitional economies occur in countries that are moving from a command economy to a market economy.

- **Now You Will Learn** China and the former Soviet Union have transitional economies.

AS YOU READ Take notes about moving to a market economy. Use the diagrams on both pages of this worksheet.

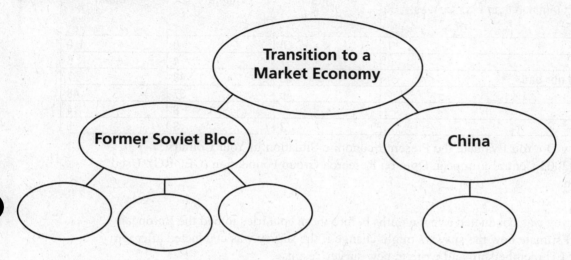

<table>
<tr><td colspan="2">VOCABULARY HUNT Circle each term where it appears in your notes and be sure you understand its meaning. If a term does not appear, write it in or next to the box where it best belongs.</td><td>privatization
perestroika</td><td>"shock therapy"
special economic zones</td></tr>
</table>

CHAPTER 18

ECONOMIC DEVELOPMENT OBJECTIVES, *CONTINUED*

APPLICATION

Mark It Up!

Survey of Economic Expectations, December 2003–January 2004			
Percent of respondents who said the economic situation in their country was . . .	Czech Republic	Hungary	Poland
Very good	0	0	0
Good	7	4	6
Neither good nor bad	35	48	27
Bad	46	37	48
Very bad	9	8	14
Don't know	3	3	5

Source: "How Do You Evaluate the Present Economic Situation in Your Country?".
Copyright © 2003 Central European Opinion Research Group Foundation (CEORG). Used
by permission.

1. This survey was conducted a few months before these countries joined the European
   Union. Estimate how the answers might change if the survey was conducted after ten
   years of EU membership and write in new survey results.

2. When they joined the European Union, how did the economies of Poland, the Czech
   Republic, and Hungary compare with those of other EU members?

   _____

   _____

3. Write two economic problems that Poland shared with Russia.

   _____

   _____

CHAPTER 18